Peter Noble

Wise
Millennial

A Field Guide to Thriving in Modern Life

"A powerful set of ruminations that are likely to hit many millennials of privilege where they live...and help start them on journeys that are likely to be both interesting and useful. *Wise Millennial* gives readers lots to think about."

Len Schlesinger, President Emeritus, Babson College;
Baker Foundation Professor, Harvard Business School

"Peter Darrow, who has been a friend for over ten years, has evolved through his life experiences to understand the depth and knowledge of what the millennial undertakes. His ability to adapt to new cities, lifestyles, and environments gives him the insight to help the young urban professional transition to changing times. Having started his own business and fostering its growth, Peter has undertaken new adventures that allow him to wisely advise on entrepreneurial endeavors. Building a brand and being the face of a business are two attributes that contribute to his acumen of wisdom. As a close personal friend, I can say that Peter's emotional intelligence is in tune with the young urban professional, and his kindness gives him the ability to empathize with young both men and women. I highly recommend his book that gives an outlook and perspective on how personal growth can lead to success."

Amy Brody Poliakoff, former cast member,
***Gallery Girls*, Bravo TV**

"Peter Darrow has compelling advice for the millennial generation formed over his short, eventful life. Having known him from his earliest days, Peter has demonstrated resilience, inner wisdom, initiative, insight, integrity, and the drive he inherited from his father, as well as the immaturity, self-discovery, recklessness, and entitlement of his privileged Upper East Side background. Through it all, he has arrived at a place of introspection and inner peace that cries out to be shared with millennials across the spectrum. Everyone his age searches for answers to life's challenges. Peter has something important to say about the quest."

George W. Madison, partner at Sidley Austin LLP and former
general counsel, US Department of the Treasury

"Peter Darrow has a relentless curiosity that borders on irksome. At least that's what I remember about being his middle school teacher at a tony East Side private school back in the mid-1990s. I have no doubt that persistence has served him well in life. I knew his father, too, as I often had to call home to discuss Peter's classroom 'enthusiasm.'"

Taylor Mali, author of *What Teachers Make: In Praise of the Greatest Job*
***in the World*, and four-time champion National Poetry Slam**

"Contrary to popular belief, millennials have it rough. They aspire to do great things and are hard on themselves, but given the constant and accelerating pace of change, millennials are also a generation without clear role models. I know Peter Darrow well, and his candid story about privilege and hardship is in many ways a tale of his generation. A funny, honest, and inspiring read."
Ned Russell, Managing Partner, Healthcare, at MDC Partners and former global client leader, Publicis Groupe

"Peter and I are both native New Yorkers and know the particular culture of the Upper East Side with its pressures and expectations. As fellow millennials, we also share in our generation's entrepreneurial spirit and desire to make a difference. What I've come to appreciate about Peter is his ability to articulate the millennial experience and his enthusiastic reminders, as we strive to achieve our dreams, about what really matters most in life."
Erin Frankel, cofounder of Jetsweat fitness app

"I was Peter's personal nutritionist while he was in grad school. I later consulted for him when he opened his restaurant, Darrow's Farm Fresh in Union Square, and I've continued to partner with him as we launch a supplement line to benefit people's health. Along the way, Peter has inspired me with his energy, passion, and enthusiasm for life, health, and wellness. Despite his affluent, privileged upbringing, he has grown into a down-to-earth and authentic guy who cares deeply about sharing his hard-won insights into how to live well from the inside out."
Julie Starr, nutritionist, wellness expert, owner of SHIFT supplements and Starr Yoga Studios

"A book that could help Peter's fellow millennials is surely needed. Many successful baby boomers were consumed by the demands of their work and tried to make up for their absence from home by showering privileges on their children, starving them of discipline. This upbringing has made many of their children ill-equipped for the challenges of today's marketplace. If Peter can show through an accurate telling of his story how he was brought up, failed at a startup, and was then changed by his failures, then this could be a valuable book."
John Tepper Marlin, PhD, president and managing member of Boissevain Books

First published in the USA in 2019 by Peter Noble Darrow

Book Design: www.adamhaystudio.com

Photography on front cover and
pages 172 and 175 by: Alejandro Cerdena

Notice of Liability

ISBN: 978-1-7336331-0-9

First Edition

www.wisemillennial.com

Dedication

To Ermie, for helping raise me. For teaching me manners and dedicating your life and love to me over 30+ years. Your prayers have been answered. I am eternally appreciative.

To Dr. Bill Carr, for teaching me that my life belongs to me.

CONTENTS

INTRODUCTION: 8
A MILLENNIAL LIBERATOR: 11
WHY READ THIS BOOK?: 14

Wise Millennial

01
CREATE YOUR OWN PATH: 18

02
CHILDREN OF AFFLUENCE: 26

03
THE INNER VOICE: 32

Healthy Millennial

04
A MILLENNIAL FACES MORTALITY: 46

05
THAT TIME I WAS VEGAN: 54

06
THE POWER OF POSITIVITY: 58

Wealthy Millennial

07
PARTY LIKE JAY GATSBY: 64

08
DARROW'S FARM FRESH: 68

09
HOW TO BURN AN INHERITANCE: 76

Social Millennial

10
FIRST LOVE LOST: 86

11
AN EPIC SECOND DATE: 90

12
HOW TO BE A DREAM MAN: 94

CONTENTS

13
REALITY DATING: 100

14
IT'S NOT YOU, IT'S NEW YORK CITY: 104

Resilient Millennial

15
THE MODERN FAMILY: 114

16
EVERYONE IS (NOT) DOING IT: 120

17
YOUR FUNDAMENTAL INSECURITY: 124

18
THE IMMORTAL GAME: 130

Adventurous Millennial

19
EYE OF A HURRICANE: 136

20
THE HONEY HUNTERS: 140

21
CHEERING FROM THE SIDELINES: 148

22
CAMP MONTAUK: 154

Instructive Millennial

23
HOW TO CRUSH COLLEGE: 162

24
BUSINESS SCHOOL AND THE VALUE OF A DEGREE: 166

25
ON MILLENNIALS: 174

Introduction

WHO THE HELL IS PETER DARROW, YOU ASK?** Allow me to introduce myself. I'm a millennial raised on the Upper East Side of Manhattan, a unique experience in and of itself. Within this storied geography, I went to elite private schools and grew up with plenty of privilege—but that affluence came at a cost to my psychological health. In my mid-twenties, my quarter-life crisis came packaged with my parents' divorce and remarriages, their dual cancer diagnoses, my father's subsequent death, inheriting and burning through a shit-ton of money, losing the girlfriend I had thought I would marry, and losing my newly founded business—all in the course of three hellish years.

Once the dust settled on what remained of my life, I had learned a few things. Like how to navigate the breakup and reassembly of my family into two households. The ins and outs of wills, trusts, and estate law—which are arguably less complicated than the personalities, behaviors, and choices of certain family members when money and property are on the line. And the sheer madness of opening and operating a large health-centric restaurant in the heart of Manhattan.

Most of all, I learned who I am deep down when all the trappings of wealth and privilege are laid bare by the reality of death. All of us who live long

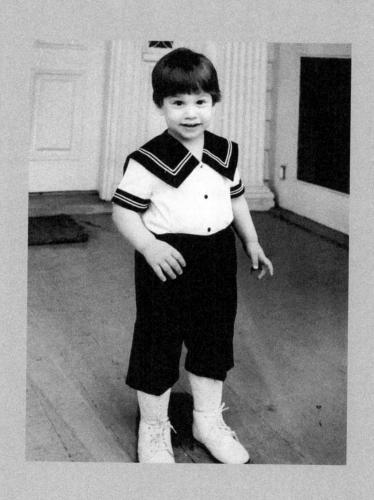

enough will eventually lose a parent, but to experience that loss prematurely is a defining moment. A shift in course. A rebuff of youthful denial. Up to that point, I had been somewhat . . . entitled. Okay, *extremely* entitled. My over-privileged sense of entitlement was partly the product of the environment in which I grew up and partly the natural qualities of a young, naïve millennial who thought he was invincible. I was not the best version of myself. But the triple whammy of losing my dad, my girlfriend, and my business became a catalyst for personal transformation the likes of which I'd never experienced before. I viewed not just all life, but all people in a vastly different light. I grew to nurture more respect, and less disdain, for things and people. I cultivated my humility and set aside my ego. It felt life-changing.

One morning not long before my thirtieth birthday, I found myself looking in the mirror and thinking to myself, *Whose life am I really living?* I was living someone else's life. Maybe my father's? It wasn't mine. Ever since I'd opened the restaurant, I woke up with nauseating headaches, feeling like the weight of the entire world rested on my shoulders. As I stared back at myself, I thought, *This must have been what it was like for my father every day.* These were the kinds of stresses my father endured—financial pressure, a relationship that fell apart, getting taken advantage of. I wondered if he, too, had felt this unhappy, if he'd regretted so many decisions he'd made in his life. Gazing into that mirror, I felt like I was looking at his ghost. In many ways, I was living his life—the life my parents envisioned for me—and not my own.

In this moment, I realized something had to change.

A Millennial Liberator

LIFE ISN'T A CONTEST BY ANY MEANS. We all deal with stuff. All of these tragedies I faced might normally happen within any person's lifespan, but for me they were condensed into an exceptionally tight time period. As a result, I've developed a deeper appreciation for what I have and the opportunities I've been given. I've been humbled, my worldview clarified. After thousands of hours of therapy, introspection, and meditation, I finally began taking control of my life and creating my own opinions, most of which have evolved far beyond my family's worldview.

I've always been rather independent, self-reflective, and critical of what I've been told. Never afraid to question myself and challenge my conceptions of the world. This inclination was only invigorated by my personal crises. Now my desire is to be a "millennial liberator"—I want to empower other young people to detach from the fucked-up values we downloaded from society and our overachieving, conforming parents and encourage them to develop a strong and healthy sense of self, something terribly lacking in today's world.

I see so many young people, especially in New York City, who are trapped in limited ways of thinking. Our minds naturally want to categorize people as good or bad, right or wrong. Perhaps this default setting of binary thinking is part of our evolutionary biology; it's what has helped our brains make quick decisions for survival. But these days, our instinctive reactions are less about physical survival and more about protecting an incredibly fragile self-image. In a world in which we can broadcast our entire lives on a tiny screen, we're being held hostage by our egos.

People can fundamentally change, but they have to *want* to change. You can't force it on anyone. People generally fear change—it makes them feel uncomfortable and insecure. They're afraid they won't be able to adapt to a new way of thinking and living. They want to go with what's comfortable instead of what's challenging. As for me, I've learned to embrace change, to become comfortable with being a little uncomfortable.

When times are easy, everything seems fine. It's only when times get tough and you hit the proverbial rock bottom that you're forced to look in the mirror and reflect on things. But it shouldn't have to be that way—we shouldn't have to *bottom out* to desire change in our lives. The goal isn't just to survive, but rather to find our true passion and deepest happiness in life.

Being independent thinkers and defining our values apart from what we've downloaded from our families and society is key to an authentic life. Too many people accept their parents' worldview like an invaluable inheritance without examining it closely. I want to challenge millennials to question everything we've ever been taught. Look at each thought, each opinion, each belief. Why do you believe the things you do? Is it just because that's "how you were raised"? Do your beliefs align with your deepest values? Do they serve you? Will you continue to maintain the status quo, or are you willing to look in the mirror and take a deep, personal assessment of yourself? This is the only way we'll grow into stronger emotional maturity and personal fulfillment.

I'm a big believer that you have the power to create your own reality; you attract the energy you put into the universe. It takes discipline and a measure of courage to take ownership of and responsibility for your decisions in order to create the life you want to live. Many people don't understand this concept—they blame their unhappiness on their job, their romantic partner, or the mistakes their parents made. But as adults, we're 100 percent responsible for our own lives now, as well as the thoughts, beliefs, and choices that brought us to this point. If what we've been doing isn't working, then it's time to take stock and shift course.

I'm a passionate advocate for this personal revolution because I sense the urgent need for change. Millennials, born between 1981 and 1996, are projected to be the largest cohort in history by 2019—we're 75 million strong, a fourth of the entire U.S. population, and we're all in the prime of our lives.

It's essential that we embrace these truths now. If you're lucky, you'll learn what life is really about eventually, but why wait until your midlife crisis to wake up? The quarter-life crisis—this moment of awakening to how stuck and disappointed and fearful you feel—is a prime opportunity to set the rest of your life on a better, fuller, more promising path.

This concept shouldn't be that hard to grasp. Millennials love to challenge existing societal norms. We love to ask, "Why?" Why does it work like that? Why does it need to be done that way? We got tired of being told we couldn't do something because "That's just the way it is." We've overturned archaic, social mores. There are no more boxes, no more boundaries. Racial diversity is a given. People are increasingly free to explore their sexuality. Gender and sexual identity are now much more fluid—gay, bisexual, transgender, non-binary, polyamorous, pansexual . . . you name it, we have it.

Societal ideas shift over time, often swinging on a pendulum. I witnessed how tough my father's generation was on themselves—nothing was ever good enough, and they always had something to prove. My dad was a workaholic, and he and his peers motivated themselves by being extremely judgmental and harsh on themselves and their children. That approach strikes me as downright masochistic.

Millennials were subjected to this behavior and its inherent emotional abuse, and now we're moving toward more compassionate ways of being. Our generation has placed our values less on materialism, money, and power and more on internal happiness and personal development. We're more likely to treat ourselves with kindness. We're more focused on natural food and holistic approaches to health. We care more about experiences than accumulating stuff. Millennials are passionate about doing work that matters to us, matches our values, and contributes to the greater good. It's a fundamental shift in our society's values and a rejection of what came before. Millennials and the upcoming Generation Z have the opportunity to create a less stressed, more balanced, happier lifestyle overall.

Why Read This Book?

ONE OF THE SIDE EFFECTS OF THE INTENSE LIFE EXPERIENCES I ENDURED IS AN ACUTE SENSE OF MY OWN MORTALITY. People in general, and millennials in particular, don't like to face this harsh aspect of reality. They prefer the bliss of denial, ignoring the inevitability of death, perhaps even thinking they will go on living forever. Though this approach may keep the psyche calm and comfortable, it leaves you with no sense of urgency.

In my case, I've been forever snapped out of such denial. I feel like I could get hit by a bus tomorrow. Our health can change with the snap of a finger. Our lives can be cut off instantly with absolutely no warning. I've already known other young people who lost their lives way too soon—they should be with us right now, but they're not. Each of us should be deeply grateful we've made it this far. Yet I look around and see so many people who seem to have it all— lots of money, a great partner, well-behaved kids, nice homes—but they're still *miserable*. Nothing is good enough for them. Their happiness is always just beyond the horizon; the closer they get to it, the farther it goes away.

My traumatic episodes forced me to understand and appreciate what really matters in life versus what doesn't. While I'm grateful for the advantages my parents granted me—growing up in an elegant home, attending upper-echelon schools, enjoying luxurious vacations—I've come to realize that none of that shit really matters. We have each been granted a certain amount of time on this earth, and we don't know how much. What are we going to do with it? What are we doing here? Now? Not to skip ahead to the big reveal, but it all comes down to living a life marked by love and compassion for others, including compassion for yourself and your parents, who, ideally speaking, did the best they could with the best of intentions. Our relationships are the most important component of our lives. As inherently social creatures, we should strive to make all our social connections authentic and meaningful—not just family relationships, but friendships and romantic partnerships as well.

The immediacy of death has brought more immediacy to life. Every moment of every waking hour is full of possibility. I love not knowing what tomorrow brings. I love waking up every day and not knowing how the day will unfold. The unpredictability is what makes life unique and special. How boring would it be if every day were the same as the last?

A rich life is one that embraces all aspects of our glorious humanity. Likewise, *Wise Millennial* is broken into sections by themes: cultivating a strong sense of self, choosing healthy habits for wellness and longevity, life as a one-percenter and why wealth isn't what it's cracked up to be, how to stay sane while dating in New York City, how to be adaptable to an ever-changing world, and how to maximize one's volume of fun and adventure.

Throughout these pages, I share stories, insights, and valuable lessons that I hope will transcend generations and personal backgrounds, thereby potentially preventing others from making similar mistakes. I want to give millennials the skills, tools, and mental framework to make more fulfilling life decisions. I also aim to be a bridge-builder, connecting older and younger generations to millennials through shared values, in hope that we can understand each other better. Most of all, I want to reassure millennials that they're not alone on this journey to becoming their own person. Everyone is entitled to happiness, and everyone has their own path to find it. But no one can live your life for you. I hope after reading this book you'll feel a sense of empowerment and a stronger connection in what can sometimes seem like a lonely world.

When you get right down to it, it doesn't have to be.

Releasing values that
no longer serve you
and building a strong
sense of self

se

Millennial

01

Create Your Own Path

I TRY TO NEVER USE THE WORD "HATE." However, there are two things in this world that I absolutely loathe, for which I have nothing but purely malicious and evil intent from the bottom of my soul: the Boston Red Sox, and cancer.

SUNDAY, MAY 19, 2013, 11 a.m.

"Come on, Dad!!" I screamed.

I rolled up the sleeves of my white Head of the Charles sweater as if I were preparing for a fight. But it wasn't my fight—it was my father's.

We were in the hallway of the critical care unit of New York Presbyterian on the Upper East Side, preparing to transfer him to another hospital in a last-ditch attempt to save his life. I caught a glimpse of my father's nearly lifeless body on the moveable gurney. His head was propped on ice packs to reduce possible brain swelling—he had flatlined earlier that morning for about ninety seconds, long enough that the doctors wanted to try to prevent any potential brain damage, should he survive at all. Though they had managed to revive him once already, we were in the middle of a very touch-and-go situation.

That morning, after the first time he coded, the doctors had managed to get him stabilized. Shortly afterward, I joined my other family members—my sister, Meredith, my stepmother, Denise, and my father's brother, Duncan,—in the waiting area, where we pretended we were doctors and brainstormed creative ideas on how to get him to survive this episode. At one point, one of the actual doctors came up to us.

18

"The situation is ominous."

I will never forget those words.

"I have an idea," he said, "but it's risky and has never really been done before. There is a special piece of machinery—the only one in the city—that can recirculate his blood while on life support."

Dad was already in a coma and not getting enough oxygen. The machine in question performed extracorporeal membrane oxygenation—a form of advanced life support that works like an artificial lung to oxygenate the bloodstream. Trying this on Dad was a Hail Mary pass of sorts, since it was incredibly risky for a patient this sick.

My family responded, "Great! Let's give it a try. What floor is the machine on?"

"Well, that's the problem," the doctor said slowly, averting his gaze. "It's at the Columbia University Medical Center on 168th Street, far uptown. We'd have to transport him and just hope he survives the transport. There's no guarantee he will."

The effort didn't seem promising, but we were willing to take the risk. We didn't feel confident about his chances if we stayed and did nothing. But while the doctors were prepping my dad for the transport, he started coding again, right there in the hallway. The medical staff rushed him into a room and barred anyone other than my stepmother from entering.

Though my sister and I waited helplessly outside, the door to his room was left ajar. I sneaked a peek. It looked like either war triage or an alien abduction—cables and wires hung all over the room, running from multiple devices to my father's dying body. Numerous electrical machines, displaying indecipherable data on their LED screens, beeped and pinged and hummed. A half dozen nurses and doctors hovered over my father and passed around different equipment like a game of speed chess.

While the frenzy swirled around her, my stepmom sat next to my father's bedside cheering him on. "Keep fighting, Peter! You can make it! Keep rowing!"

After a treacherous five minutes that felt like an eternity, the medical team managed to stabilize him once again. Should he actually make it through, however, none of us knew what mental condition he would be in long-term, if there even would be a long-term. But that was like making it to the World Series; in the moment, we were just focused on the playoffs.

In 2001, my paternal grandmother died from lung cancer, and then in 2008 my father, Peter V. Darrow, was diagnosed with end-stage multiple myeloma, a type of blood cancer that attacks the plasma cells, white blood cells that fight infection and illness. Only three months later, my mother was diagnosed with stage-one breast cancer. My mother's treatment—a lumpectomy, chemotherapy, and radiation—was ultimately successful, and she's in good health and high spirits today.

My father, on the other hand, battled his disease for four years. The first moment he realized something was wrong was while he was rowing on the ergomoter (indoor rower) at the gym. My dad loved to row; he first started rowing in 1968 with Columbia's lightweight rowing team. Around the time he was diagnosed with cancer, he got his old college crew together again to row the Head of the Charles Regatta in Boston. These old geezers who hadn't rowed in thirty years came together and started an annual tradition. They rowed the Charles every year for about seven years, until he passed, and then the guys continued the tradition in my dad's honor for another five years afterward.

That day at the gym while my dad was rowing on the erg, he felt pain in his chest as if he had broken a rib. Tests later revealed a tumor the size of a grapefruit in his chest cavity. Following surgery to remove the cancerous mass, Dad underwent aggressive chemotherapy and radiation. Though he went into remission, the cancer came back twice. The first time, he had a stem-cell transplant using his own harvested stem cells. When the cancer returned two years later, a second transplant used donor stem cells.

Normally doctors inject donor stem cells all at once, but in order to reduce the chance of rejection or graft versus host disease, they planned to try a radical new treatment of slowly reintroducing the T cells in stages. Between the operation and the first round of T cell injections was about a six-month period in which Dad could not get sick. But he did get sick. To this day, I think what killed my father was that he wasn't willing to take a break to allow himself to recover—he was just back to business as usual. He went to work and traveled when he should have been at home wearing a mask to shield himself from germs.

When you have a stem-cell transplant, you have no immunity. You have zero white blood cells, so you have no defense from the outside world. But my father wasn't the kind of guy who could just sit still and relax. When he was about three weeks away from that first round of T cells, he developed a bacterial infection, which quickly turned into pneumonia. A healthy person could have taken antibiotics to help the body fight it off, but no antibiotic known to man was strong enough for my dad in his condition. It was too late. He first went into the hospital on a Wednesday, and by Sunday my family was keeping vigil during his final hours.

After the second time my dad coded, the medical staff waited a short while to ensure he remained stable. The transport between the two hospitals was a delicate balancing act, given the volume of tubes and machines keeping my dad alive, but the hospital team managed to get him downstairs and into an ambulance, and then drove him to the hospital uptown where he was hooked up to the ECMO machine.

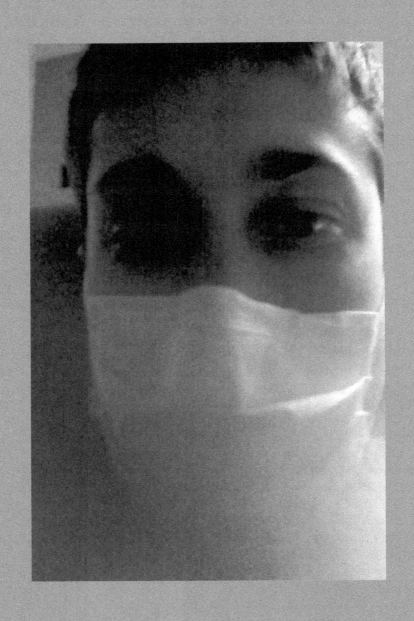

We exhausted all our options, but in the end it wasn't enough.

I entered the room where my dad was still hooked up to the machine and had the hardest conversation I would ever have in my life: I had to say goodbye to my father. I wondered what to say, knowing this would be the last time I ever saw him. He was in a coma—could he actually hear me? I told him how much I loved him and what a great dad he had been. I told him he had raised two beautiful children who would continue to make him proud.

What else do you say? What else *can* you say? In that moment, I realized how many life events he wouldn't live to witness. Weddings, the birth of his grandchildren—all of these future moments flashed in front of my eyes. It was a crazy thing to feel. An out-of-body experience. The pain of that one-way conversation will live with me forever.

I left the hospital and headed downtown to meet my mother for dinner. She had been living in Minneapolis since she remarried, but she'd flown into town to be with Meredith and me. At about a quarter to eight, while we were eating our main course, my sister called.

"Dad just passed away."

The sights and sounds of the restaurant around me faded away. All I saw was my father in that hospital bed—the intubation tube down his throat, the feeding tube up his nose, the IVs pierced into his arms, the various bodily fluids, the desperate last moments before death. Those images are burned onto my retinas, and I will never forget them.

My father was only sixty-two when he died. He was incredibly kind, compassionate, and intelligent, and the most passionate man I ever met. He worked as a partner in a major international law firm for nearly thirty years, and his relentless dedication to his career made him extremely successful and well-respected in his field. He certainly didn't deserve to get cancer, but he never complained. When I gave a eulogy at his funeral, one thing I said was how incredibly impressed I was that, after their diagnoses, neither of my parents ever asked, "Why me?" or, "Why is life so unfair?" Instead, they asked, "Okay, what's the next step?" They just stayed focused on the next hurdle ahead of them. Their strength and courage inspired me and served as an example to follow.

While I loved my father, our relationship was a complicated one. As his son, I looked up to him for strength, stability, support, and moral guidance. The millennial generation was born to baby boomers, who were themselves raised by men who had served in World War II. America was a very different place then, especially when it came to beliefs about child-rearing and psychological development. Many men of that generation—my father and his peers included—felt that in order to set an example for young boys, they had to challenge us with emotional hardiness, or "tough love." Some of the dads I've known have displayed disappointment, anger, or lack of empathy when their sons cried, as if showing any feelings were a sign of weakness.

Growing up, I experienced this dynamic during soccer practice, Little League baseball games, and even chess tournaments. When kids made a mistake or were defeated in competition, their dads yelled at them relentlessly. Forget saying something encouraging like, "Well, you did the best you could." Maybe a condolence and the participation trophy were offered up at the end, but not until heaps of guilt had been dished out.

My father often said to me, "Peter, I may not be the smartest guy in the room, but I certainly will be the hardest working." Though I might argue this wasn't the healthiest or most emotionally balanced philosophy, it reflected my father's admirable work ethic and determination for success. He communicated to me what he believed was important. After he died, I wondered where to go for guidance now that he was gone. What was I supposed to do once my life was left with such a huge void?

The scary and hard answer was this: seek it from within. I realized that for the first time in my life, in my father's absence, I got to create my own unique path. I could become my own person. I could learn to rely on myself rather than rely on others for insight and guidance. I could be whoever I wanted to be and create my own reality. That reality might be consistent with my father's, or it might be wildly different. Either way, it was up to me.

An interesting observation came to me after my father passed away. I felt like I needed to be "the man of the house"—that somehow it became my responsibility to be the emotional stronghold and decision-maker for my other family members, speaking vicariously on my dad's behalf. This expectation robbed me of my voice and sidelined my own mourning process. It became an incredible burden, and in hindsight I recognize how futile and unnecessary it was. But I felt as if the torch had been passed to me, and at age twenty-six, I had to rise to the challenge.

Even after my father died, I felt like I had to prove myself to him and win his acceptance. I heard his voice in my head: "Peter, I don't agree with this decision." "Peter, why are you at the gym at three o'clock? You should be working." A constant guilt trip, as if I weren't allowed to do things my way even now that I was on my own. I found myself standing in the gym having thirty-minute arguments in my head with a dead person! If my father were alive today, I'd ask, "Dad, are you happy with the outcome? Given that you know the end result, would you have changed anything about your life or lived it differently, maybe with less stress?" I suspect he'd respond, "No, Peter, because I raised a beautiful family with two amazing kids I'm very proud of."

That was the frustrating part. I couldn't have another live conversation with him. I couldn't ask him, "Dad, why did you think that way?" or, "Why did you think it was okay to say those things to me that one time?" I remembered the positive aspects of our relationship, like the Yankees games and the regattas and the weekends he visited me at boarding school, but I also got hung up on the negatives, like the expectations for excellence as dictated by the norms and mores of Upper East Side society. It was stifling. We often try to live our lives based on our parents' expectations. It fascinates me to hear people say, "Well, that's just how I was raised." Just because our parents *raised* us a certain way doesn't mean we're required to continue believing what they taught us. When your parents aren't there anymore, whose expectations are you playing to?

Losing a parent taught me that I get to decide which qualities and lessons from my childhood I'm going to keep and which ones I'm going to let go of as I move forward. After my dad died, I could no longer live my life according to what others thought I should be doing or even what I thought I should be doing. I realized there is no "should." You have to live your life organically according to what's best and truest for you.

This is the theme of my life: *we* get to decide what is right or wrong for us—no one else. But be sure to make it count. What good is earning all the money in the world if you die at fifty-five of a heart attack? Or at sixty-two of a rare and deadly cancer? Life is short enough already, even when you're healthy, and health can change so fast. Death feels all too real to me, but it also has added a lot of value to the business of actually living. I appreciate being alive every single day. This may seem like an easy thing to say, but only hard experiences can make you truly believe it to your core.

What's funny is that I used to feel obligated to say, "Of course I would trade anything to have my father back." But I'm not so sure. I no longer feel obligated to say that, not because I don't love him or I somehow wish him dead. Of course it's not that! Rather, it's because I feel liberated. There's no one to judge me. There's no one to critique me anymore. Not that anyone should have to go to the extreme of losing someone to have that mental separation, but, for me, the only way I was ever going to get out from under my father's shadow was for him to no longer be there, as unfortunate as that is.

I feel like I've been given an opportunity to finally become my own person. And I would never have learned these lessons if my father hadn't passed away. So now I'm moving forward with compassion toward my father and appreciation of the incredible opportunities he gave me. I'm creating my own path and my own definition of success. My father often said, "Peter, you will only be successful at the things you're passionate about."

I agree, Dad. That's just the kind of life I'm all about.

02

Children of Affluence

AS MILLENNIALS NEAR THE AGE WHEN THEY'LL BECOME PARENTS THEMSELVES, IT IS OF THE UTMOST IMPORTANCE TO EXAMINE SOME DOS AND DON'TS TO AVOID MAKING THE MISTAKES OF OUR PARENTS' GENERATION . . . AND MAKING NEW ONES IN THE PROCESS. Personally, I grew up with highly motivated and educated parents who both worked in financial services. My father was a corporate lawyer in a major law firm for more than thirty years, and my mom worked in investment banking for more than twenty years before switching to the nonprofit sector. These are some insights I share on the ever-controversial and sensitive topic of parenting.

Want to know how to piss a parent off no matter how good of a mood they're in? Tell them how to raise their child. It's pretty comical, to be honest, to see how you can get someone from zero to 100 in two seconds. That's the nature of the sensitivity of this subject. Obviously, there's no manual for how to be the best parents, but I believe there are some basic lessons to be learned from my personal experience. My intent here is not to take out any frustrations on my existing family members (that's what psychotherapy is for!), but as well-intentioned as parents are, we must understand one basic principle: *all parents wound their children.*

The question therefore isn't whether or not there's such a thing as a perfect parent. We know for a fact there isn't. The question then becomes, "What was the extent of the damage, and what steps have been taken to heal the wounds since its occurrence?" Most parents strategically raise their kids in one of two ways: 1) they model styles similar to those of their parents and how they were raised, thus perpetuating the same issues over multiple generations, or 2) to the extent that there is any deviation from the first, they raise their kids by the standards and rules to which they want them to conform, but not necessarily those that are in the best interest of the child. This latter point is generally made when there is a failure to acknowledge that the child is, believe it or not, unique, with a different set of interests than your own. Crazy to think, I know, given you share the same genes and all.

Allow me to personalize this for a moment. As I mentioned, I was very fortunate and humbled to have grown up with two loving, caring, highly motivated and financially successful parents. A very lucky childhood indeed. In addition to my two wonderful parents, I was also raised by our live-in nanny, Hyacinth "Ermie" Springer. She was a native of Barbados (a former British colony in the West Indies) and helped raise me starting at one year old. She worked with our family for more than twenty-five years and taught me many of the manners I have today. Very uniquely, one could suggest that I was raised (in part) by a black woman from Barbados, with some British formalities. Regardless, as I enter my thirties and reflect back on my upbringing, I recognize that in certain aspects, I have important ideological differences from my parents and the way they raised me. For example, there were circumstances where my parents were highly judgmental of others based on their wealth or educational background. There was a certain formula—if you didn't go to certain schools or belong to certain private social clubs or work for specific companies, then you weren't "successful." That's what I call conditional love. I cannot emphasize this next point enough: it wasn't malicious or intentional in any way. It was probably with the best of intentions. This is just what had worked for *them*. It was a projection of their own parents' insecurities. Naturally, they assumed this would also work for their child. It stemmed from a combination of concern and love.

But just because they raised me in a certain way doesn't mean I necessarily agree with it. I often look back and think to myself, "You know, that comment they made was pretty fucked up. I don't believe that now, and it's not reflective of my core values." Moreover, I don't need to subject myself to the same set of rules my parents believe in. I don't need to stress when I break some rule in my head that doesn't belong to me, because I get to create my own rules. Instead of feeling angry or frustrated, I've learned to have compassion. They were doing the best they could. I don't hold that against them.

At some point, you really have to ask yourself what's more important, the cookie-cutter way you envision your child's future, or their happiness? Because sometimes there's not a correlation between the two. You can send them to all the private schools you want. You can make them work hundreds of hours to kick ass on their SATs. You can push them into a posh junior position at your friend's Upper East Side law firm. But at what point in all this intense parental planning do you stop and ask yourself the most basic questions: Does this make them happy? Is this what *they* want, or what *I* want?

I can't tell you how many of my wealthy family friends are depressed. Money does *not* buy happiness. Happiness comes from within. These high-rolling partners, CEOs, and veritable Facebook fanboys may be making fortunes, but fortunes can't buy an end to their own inner turmoil. The specter of their parents' expectations still haunts them like their own shadow, following them everywhere they go. Perhaps in their depression—their feelings of inadequacy—they've resorted to drugs and alcohol. The more money they have, the easier it is to fuel their addictions—and the easier it is to hide them.

Perhaps this hypothetical, now-miserable CEO had grown up with aspirations to become a painter. Not even a famous one, just a painter. He grew up with a supreme love of drawing, which later evolved into an obsession with oil paints that, just shy of eating them, would have put Van Gogh to shame. It was his dream. His *passion*. Remember what my father said? *You'll only be successful at the things you're passionate about.* The CEO has several million dollars in his bank account, but if he's not happy doing what he does, he's not successful. This path didn't start when he graduated college and entered the workforce. It likely started back when he was a young child, watching his parents plot his own future for him.

So, what's the lesson here? First off, what might be best for you isn't necessarily best for your child. It's important to take into consideration their unique interests and passions, regardless of whether or not they align with your own. Acknowledge that their core values may be wildly different than your own. They're a separate, unique human being.

Secondly, the goal in parenting is not to try to prevent your kid from making mistakes, as much as we want to, but rather to be there as a safety net for when they do fail, and to prevent them from falling too far down the hole by themselves. The goal should be, in some ways, to *encourage* failure. I know that sounds ludicrous. But it's only through failure that we learn life's most powerful lessons. It's okay to fail. And we should let our children know that when they do, we'll be here to catch them. Don't come down hard on them because they failed, but focus on the reason why they failed. There's a fundamental difference between the two.

The last observation worth noting is concerning codependent

relationships. You're a *parent*. You're not your child's best friend. Some moms (mostly single ones) want to be their daughter's best friend and do everything together. And I'm not trying to sound naïve in understanding the unique bond that a mother shares with her daughter, for it is a special one indeed. The problem here is that boundaries easily get blurred, and it can be confusing and have detrimental effects on the child down the road. Most commonly, this manifests itself in "failure to launch" scenarios, where the child is both emotionally and physically dependent upon their parent into their late twenties and thirties. This can cause emotional and relationship stress, and identity confusion for the child.

Moms, I know you love your daughters. That's great. But it's not okay to be going to a nightclub with her, or inviting her to fancy, expensive charity galas just because you don't have a date. Know the boundaries and stick to them even if you don't want to—kind of like wanting to eat that entire pint of ice cream at 1 a.m. Delicious in the moment, but not the best move long-term.

This doesn't just apply to mothers, either. The same thing happens between fathers and sons but under different circumstances. For example, my father always wanted me to be just like him. He wanted me to work eighty-hour weeks, to join a law firm, to be successful and determined at all times. As a direct result, this required me to shadow his work ethic, to listen to his rants on the meaning of success and how *exactly* I was going to get there (under his tutelage, of course). It meant talking business or politics at the dinner table when I just wanted to talk about my friends or my day at school. Although it's not the same as mom wanting to impose on her daughter's first date, it's still an example of invading a child's space.

Let your child be their own person, and give them the space to be themselves.

03

The Inner Voice

OUTSIDE OF OUR FAMILIES, THE INSTITUTIONS THAT EDUCATE US TEND TO BE AN EXTENSION OF OUR PARENTS' VALUES AND TEACH US TO CONFORM. In this chapter, I share my experiences attending elite private schools in Manhattan and going off to boarding school at St. Paul's School at age fourteen, and how I only saw in hindsight what kind of mental and social conditioning these institutions were instilling in me and my classmates. To truly develop a healthy sense of self, we have to listen to our own inner voice of wisdom and live closely aligned to our own sense of truth and goodness—not what society (especially affluent society) deems best for us. One of the ways I ultimately rebelled against these constraints was by choosing to attend the University of Miami in South Florida—the polar opposite of the culture and geography of my upbringing—as a way of breaking free.

I attended Trevor Day School for kindergarten and first grade before switching to the Browning School on the Upper East Side of Manhattan (62nd, between Park and Madison Avenue, to be precise) for second through eighth grade.

Before we proceed, I think it's important to educate you on the range of

schools within this ecosystem. Within this list exists a great deal of conflict about which schools are the best. I'm not going to list them by perceived rank; I'll leave that snobbery to the admissions folks and parents of Manhattan. And by no means is this list exhaustive, so please don't sue me if I missed your school.

All-Boys Schools:	All-Girls Schools:	Coed Schools:
Browning	Spence	Trinity
St. David's	Chapin	Dalton
St. Bernard's	Marymount	Poly Prep
Collegiate	Hewitt	Horace Mann
Allen Stevenson	Sacred Heart	Riverdale
Buckley	Nightingale	Birch Wathen Lenox
	Brearley	Trevor Day

I can't really speak for the co-ed schools, because it's a very different experience in terms of classroom environment and size. They seem to operate as an entirely different class. But as for the single-sex schools, I can reveal more information. First, you have to understand that these schools are tiny. The entire school generally operates within a single standalone New York City brownstone building. In case you don't know, brownstone buildings used to be single-family homes for the wealthy in the early part of the twentieth century.

We're talking K–12, around 300 students total. Generally, twenty to forty kids comprise an entire grade, divided into sub-sections of ten to twenty students each. Except for lunch, you're with the same ten students all day, every day, for most of your entire youth. That's what you're paying for as a parent. The small size, attention, and close supervision of *your child*. Sounds great to the parent, but to the child? Not so much. You can't get away with much nonsense. You're more easily subjected to getting into trouble and (*gasp*) getting sent to the principal's office. But the theme is conformity, and the paying parents have no problem with any of this.

Turtlenecks were permissible until fifth grade, when we were required to wear a blazer and tie. Every morning as I entered the building, I'd shake the headmaster's hand (creates a nice sense of community, no?). If I was late more than five times per semester, I'd get automatic detention. Every boy's school had a partner "sister school" (ours was Hewitt), and there would be arranged coed dances called Goddard Gaieties. Many parents would even go so far as to sign their children up for ballroom-style dance lessons called Barclays. What a great place to meet your future spouse when you're at the ripe age of ten. Consider it a modern high-society version of the arranged marriage. And trust me, parents get *very* into it.

There are pros and cons to private schools. What you're really paying for in a private school education are a few things. First is the attention to detail given to individual students. While it's possible to "slip through the cracks" as a child in a private school, I'm willing to bet it's statistically rare. A higher percentage of teachers and faculty really do go the extra mile to make sure each and every student is keeping pace with the curriculum. They at least seem to be genuinely engaged and interested in the success of their students.

While there are many fantastic public schools with equally fantastic teachers, there are also a few teachers on tenure who aren't as motived as they should be. Given all the protections that tenure provides, it can be damaging to the overall student culture. It goes without saying that I'm biased, but if every six out of ten public school teachers are exceptional, I'm willing to bet that every eight out of ten private school teachers are exceptional, given the vetting process and low tolerance of BS from the administration and parents. So, you tell me, what is that extra 20 percent worth to you? A couple hundred grand?

As I mentioned earlier, what you're really paying for is a "heightened sensitivity" environment in which parents and faculty are freaking out about Johnny being late multiple times, or using a curse word, or teasing another student. There is almost zero tolerance for big-deal items like bullying, bringing drugs to school, skipping class, and so on. Let's not be naïve—this still goes on in private schools. Kids are just more adept at hiding it. These are the holes in many public schools that everyone works hard to close. But I believe somewhere along this "everything needs to be perfect" path in which adults can get lost, there is a detrimental disregard for the thoughts, desires, and harmless pleasures of adolescence. All that individual attention can be great when you're young, but it can have adverse effects in your high school years.

There needs to be a balance. Stop doing Johnny's homework for him. I know how much you want your child to get an A, but this thesis clearly wasn't written by an eight-year-old. Stop being such a control freak about who your child plays with, which park they go to, what they wear all the time, and when they're allowed to watch TV. These actions undoubtedly stem from good intentions, but be careful. I know many "alpha parents" whose children end up completely rebelling against everything they were taught simply because they got burnt out and were tired of living their life according to what everyone else wanted. It can rob them of their individuality; it can rob them of their childhood.

I know kids who had every opportunity in life and pissed it away simply because they had no sense of freedom. I've seen many tattoos, lots of experimentation with drugs, and a gross lack of career motivation. I even know a kid who died tragically before his time. Thrust into this preppy lifestyle over which they have absolutely no control, children become alienated to a dangerous degree, which pushes them toward drugs, alcohol, and depression. I wish I were making this up, but the reality is that it happens far too often. It's easy to read this and glance over it without much thought, but please, try to take my words seriously. This is a real thing, and it could easily happen to your child. What's your ROI on that?

At a private school, you're also paying for empowerment. We all recognize that knowledge is power. However, for reasons I don't fully understand, a greater emphasis seems to be placed on this notion in private school environments than public schools. Despite the conformity, the idea that you can create your own success by being taught to critically analyze, question, and change the world around you is emphasized among the private school crowd. "You are going to be the change-makers in society," the teachers say. Of course, this isn't to say this sort of message doesn't exist in public school environments. I'm sure there are numerous incredible teachers and parents who promote this kind of independent thought in public schools. It just appears to be slightly less prevalent.

Do you need to send your kid to a private school? Can your son or daughter receive an equal, if not better, education at public school? I would say it really depends on the neighborhood and the quality of the school system in your district. There are many bad public schools (and private schools), but there are also many fine ones, and, all things being equal, your child probably has the same exact chance of future success without you having to drop several hundred grand on their education. Who the hell thinks every financially successful person came out of a private school? That's ridiculous. But if you have the financial means, and it helps you sleep a little better at night thinking you've put your child under "better" adult supervision during the day, by all means, go for it. You can't put a price on great sleep, am I right?

BOARDING SCHOOLS

After my time at Browning, I attended St. Paul's, a boarding school in Concord, New Hampshire. Upon reflection, it was a very impactful time in my life. I get asked a lot, "Peter, knowing what you know now, would you do it all over again, and would you send your kids to boarding school?" It's such a seemingly simple and innocuous question, but it has a complex answer. Here is my response:

This part is probably the hardest emotionally for me to write. It's not because I have something to hide, nor did anything particularly traumatic happen to me. But the teenage years, especially between the ages of fourteen and eighteen, are critical in shaping your worldview. As anyone can attest, these are powerful years in a young person's development. Your brain is literally transforming.

I could write an entire book on boarding schools (and many people have). But to try to be concise for your reading, I'm going to break this into three short sections. I'm not going to go into much detail about day-to-day life in a boarding school, nor will I delve into the easily approachable and juicy subject of scandals (there are plenty of books and *Vanity Fair* articles you can read for that). It's not that I'm afraid to talk about those things, or even that I don't want to. It's just that they've been covered ad nauseum and aren't very exciting for me anymore. I want to go deeper than that. I want to explore the psychological and emotional impact that such institutions have on a fourteen-year-old who's never lived away from home before. Why is no one talking about that? Oh, that's right. It's not a sexy headline. It doesn't sell papers or lead to online clicks. That's why.

Before people misinterpret this chapter as me railing against boarding school, which I'm absolutely not doing, let me say this: boarding school can serve a great purpose. It teaches a young person to become independent at a young age. There's no more relying on Mommy and Daddy. If you dig a hole for yourself, you must dig yourself out. Simple. Also, it provides a wonderful avenue through which teenagers can reach and exceed their intellectual potential more than they ever thought possible. It pushes, stimulates, and challenges you emotionally. Boarding school can also provide a safe environment to express yourself and pursue creative talents, with incredible resources that many colleges and universities could only dream of providing their students. That's the good news. Now let's look at some of the bad.

01

CONFLICTS OF INTEREST
AND STUDENT CONFUSION

In loco parentis. It's Latin, meaning "in place of parents." It's also a central theme of St. Paul's (and many other boarding schools). They proudly preach the line to all incoming students and their respective parents, the idea being, "Don't worry, your kids are safe with us. We have their best interests at heart, on your behalf."

At my boarding school, there was a faculty member by the name of Reverend Anthony Campbell. Keep in mind, it's a traditionally Episcopal school, so we had faculty members who were also part of the church. We met in a chapel four days a week for an all-school morning meeting in which various members of the school community would be invited to give inspiring speeches to the student body, along with general announcements.

Reverend Campbell was a heavy-set black man with a deep and

powerful voice. He was also incredibly inspiring; he would often deliver motivational sermons during morning chapel, which never failed to capture the attention of even the sleepiest of students. He was a rare figure; any time he spoke, you listened. He even made several appearances on CNN to discuss a range of topics.

One day in 2002, when I was a sophomore, it was announced during morning chapel that Reverend Anthony Campbell had tragically passed away from a massive heart attack. I had never actually introduced myself to Reverend Campbell, nor had he taught any of my classes. I only knew him through his powerful sermons. Emotionally distraught, I wasn't sure how to react. I decided to write a letter to his family explaining how much he had inspired me, despite never actually meeting the man. I emailed a copy of the letter to two people: my advisor at the time, who also happened to be a chaplain of the school, and another faculty member, the head chaplain. I asked if they would please forward my letter to Reverend Campbell's family.

The next day I received a direct reply back from the head chaplain. He loved the letter, and he wanted me to deliver it as a morning speech to the entire school. I was in complete awe, humbled by his request. I immediately accepted the invitation. My intention in writing the letter was never to deliver it to the school, or to anyone, for that matter. It was purely written from my heart, which had been moved by the sudden death and my sadness that I would never get to hear Reverend Campbell's chapel speeches ever again. But I was excited to speak to my school—I felt it was a unique opportunity to connect.

Fast forward one week. I was a few days away from delivering my letter to the entire school, and my advisor called me into his office to pull the plug on the whole thing. He said, "Peter, I don't feel it's appropriate for you to give this speech. Morning speeches are traditionally reserved for upperclassmen, and you're only a sophomore. I'm sorry, but I can't allow this to proceed."

The news was earth-shattering. I had poured my heart out in that letter. And though I did it with the sole intention of sending goodwill to the family of a much-beloved man, after the invitation I felt as though one of the deepest, most fundamental aspects of my being (compassion) had been validated. Furthermore, it was going to be presented in front of the whole school. I'd mentally and emotionally prepared for such a speech. I probably grew more in that week alone than I had all year. And then at the eleventh hour, my advisor delivered this devastating blow—that I was not allowed to speak and that, due to my age, I had obviously not earned the right.

Have you ever been so excited to do something that put you in an extremely vulnerable state, only to have the wind wrenched from your sails? Yes, you have. And it teaches you a lot, doesn't it? It teaches you that sometimes, when you show your inner self, it can get crushed by outside forces. The result? You retreat further and further inside, unwilling to show your true self for fear of being hurt. That's what I learned that day.

I couldn't believe it. I was so upset, but being only fifteen years old, I was afraid to challenge my advisor. I didn't want to mess with more than 150 years of school tradition and risk getting into bigger trouble or being asked to leave. My experience at St. Paul's was never the same after that. Moving forward, I felt unwanted and unappreciated. I retreated into myself.

To this day, my biggest regret is not speaking up. *In loco parentis,* right? In place of parents. When you're young, you take so much at face value. You don't know what you don't know. If an adult tells you, "That's the way it is," you have no grounds to question it. Why would you? They have your best interests at heart. But here's the reality: the faculty have their own superiors to report to, and their own agenda. It's their job to represent the best interests of the *institution.* Sometimes this can align with the student's interests, sometimes not. You think you're receiving information that's in your best interest, but you're not. You're receiving information that's in the best interest of the school. This mixed messaging can be very confusing for a child, and potentially very damaging. Knowing what I know now, and having this gained perspective, I should have immediately called into question this conflict of interest and escalated it to the president of the school. Hell, I should have gone up and given the speech anyway. What's harmful about giving a kid an opportunity to share his reflections on a prominent faculty member's recent death? Nothing.

This story is specific, but I assure you, it serves as a microcosm for many other instances where this kind of conflict in interests has occurred. I can't offer any guidance on how to change it; it kind of comes with the territory of a school culture steeped in tradition. But it is something to be acutely aware of. Ultimately, I learned a very valuable lesson early in life that is worth taking note of: Don't be afraid to speak up. Don't necessarily trust others to have your best interests in mind. People have agendas of their own. They're just people, like everyone else. If you really want something, you have to fight for it. No one is going to do it for you.

UNDERSTANDING THE SYSTEM

In order to appreciate these remarks, you must first have an understanding of the whole picture of these historic boarding schools. These "elite" boarding schools, as the press loves to call them, are very old, and steeped in money and tradition.

THE INNER VOICE

In no particular order, and by no means exhaustive:

Groton	Middlesex	Choate
Hotchkiss	Kent	Taft
Lawrenceville	Exeter	Andover
Deerfield	St. Paul's	

They interconnect in both athletic and academic "leagues", to list a few:

Athletic

Academic

SSL – Six School's League

ESA – Eight Schools Association

ISL – Independent School League

Ten Schools Admission Organization

MAPL – Mid-Atlantic Prep League

Founders League

The endowment at St. Paul's is over $560 million in investments, with total net assets at slightly under $800 million. Not too shabby (but much less than Phillips Exeter, with total assets well over a billion). These eleven high schools listed here have endowments which collectively total $5.7 billion. Let's not forget, we're talking about high schools here. Not venture capital firms. *High schools.*

These schools are historically very focused on students' admission into Ivy League colleges. If I'm not mistaken, a long time ago, if your son (prior to the schools turning coed) attended one of these high schools, you could call up Harvard, Yale, or Princeton and reserve a spot for your child four years in the future. To verify this, I had fun looking at an old St. Paul's yearbook from 1936. I'm going to type out what I read from the graduating high school class, completely unaltered in any way (if you don't believe me, go to the school library and request a copy yourself to follow along).

In order, from the top: *Harvard, Yale, Yale, Princeton, Princeton, Yale, Princeton, Bowdoin, Harvard, Williams, California Institute of Technology, Princeton, Yale, Princeton, Yale, MIT, Yale, Yale, Princeton, Harvard, Yale, Harvard, Yale, Yale* (would you like me to keep going?), *Princeton, Princeton, Princeton, Harvard, Princeton, Princeton, Princeton, MIT, Princeton, Princeton, Yale* ... okay, I'll stop.

Pretty impressive, right? I don't state any of this as a negative judgment. In fact, it's definitely something to be celebrated. Most schools would love to be able to have this history as an advertisement. I only provide this information to give the 99.99 percent of people who didn't have the good fortune to attend one of these schools a little insight into the kind of beast we're dealing with here. It's a mammoth one. It's also important to understand that St. Paul's is an "all-boarding" environment (one of very few remaining in the country), meaning everyone lives on campus all the time; there are zero "day students" (those who go to class during the day on campus, but return

41

home at the end of each day). There are limits to how often and when you're allowed to leave campus, and everything requires prior approval. This might seem like a subtle difference, but trust me, it changes the whole dynamic. It makes it a much more controlled environment. You know everyone who lives on campus, and, conversely, you know instantly when you see a new face that doesn't belong.

Where am I going with all this? I impart this information to emphasize the incredible influence and pressure put on students who attend these prestigious schools. They face not only immense pressure to perform well academically, but also to conform to the combined interests of the school administration, parents, peers, and the thousands of established living (and deceased) alumni. When a student gets in trouble for doing something, little effort is made in trying to teach the student *why* what they did is wrong. Hopefully the student learns a lesson, but no one is really focused on providing deeper context as to why a certain rule exists or the importance of upholding it.

Rather, the primary objective is to teach the student, "Never do this again, or else bad things will happen." It's a conformist, fear-based system. This is an unfortunate missed opportunity to really teach students and provide them context to understand boundaries and why they exist in the first place. I'm not suggesting that real lessons aren't learned or that faculty don't care. But this is the system we're fed into and the culture that has existed since the founding of these private institutions. Again, it's not always in our best interest, but in theirs.

03

PROTECT THE REPUTATION—AT ALL COSTS

While it's nice to have rich tradition, culture, and reputation (all great core values Americans love to talk about), sometimes these things can work against you. When you have too much of them, it can be easy to become overly focused on trying to defend them. You can lose perspective and become obsessive. Boasting a gleaming reputation, for example, is like a drug of sorts—you can't give it up. You'll do anything to keep it and to get even more.

That's why it came as no surprise to me when all these sex scandals broke in the news recently, dating back from the 1960s and '70s, including that of my old boarding school, St. Paul's, which was referred to in a recent lawsuit as a "haven for sexual predators." I even had an awkward, albeit very minor incident with a former faculty member. An inappropriate remark that should have never been made to me. I'm not focused on the disgusting details of these scandals, but the question of why this happened in the first place. What was happening culturally in our world that allowed this to persist, the pattern repeating over and over again? The answer, in my humble opinion, is a simple and dangerous sense of entitlement. It's the sense that we must "protect the reputation of the school above all else" and sweep things under the rug. Deal with them internally, quickly and quietly.

This lack of transparency is a generational issue. Born into the advent of Facebook, Twitter, and a digital world in general, millennials value transparency more than any previous generation. Instead of facing the reality that inappropriate conduct was happening, older generations have chosen to protect the reputation of the institution, hoping that in the long run it would lead to a better outcome in terms of fundraising, matriculation, and reputation.

In fairness, this trick did actually work for thirty to forty years, until suddenly the shit hit the fan. That's what happens when you try to conceal things; it'll be exponentially worse in the long run. Ironic, isn't it? All these boarding schools that like to preach such values as honesty and transparency to students don't hold themselves to the same standard. I'm sure there are some people reading this right now who aren't happy with what I'm saying. But to be honest, I have no agenda here. I'm simply calling a spade a spade. While I dislike these scandals as much as any other alumnus, I find it difficult to sympathize. This is the result of decades of poor decision-making. I only hope these schools learn their lesson this time around; you can still be relevant, influential, and powerful in today's academic circles without acting entitled. Face the music, admit your mistakes, make systemic changes, and move on.

So, to get back to the original question: "Knowing what you know now, would you do it all over again, and would you send your kids to boarding school?" My answer: I would sit my kid down, as I wish someone who had gone through the process had done with me, and fully explain to them what they were about to get themselves into. And to the extent that a fourteen-year-old can understand the context, I'd allow them to make the decision independently as to whether or not they should attend. Personally, I'm glad I had the opportunity to attend such a fine and historic institution. Truly humbled. But would I sign up for another four years? Probably not.

As a majority of millennials hit their late twenties and early thirties, the invincibility of youth makes way for the reality of mortality

Heal

thy Millennial

04

A Millennial Faces Mortality

IN 2010, I SUFFERED A PARASITIC INFECTION KNOWN AS OCULAR TOXOPLASMOSIS IN MY LEFT EYE. For more than three weeks, I was essentially blind in one eye. After aggressive steroid treatment, the ophthalmologist was thankfully able to reduce the intraocular inflammation and eventually return my vision clarity to normal levels. However, there remains a small, permanent "blind spot" in my eye. Toxoplasmosis is actually one of the most common parasites in the world, despite very low public awareness. This experience taught me what it felt like to (temporarily) have one eye, but more importantly, it taught me a very humbling lesson in one's health.

I sat on the plane, barely able to keep my eyes open. I had just spent the weekend partying in Miami and was sitting on the tarmac waiting to fly back to New York City. My body felt rundown and beat up from the excessive drinking at loud nightclubs. I was twenty-four years old and still trying to figure my life out, but otherwise perfectly healthy without a care in the world. I was still residing in the pipe dream of invincibility. I was young, strong, healthy. Nothing could defeat me. Naïve innocence, you might say. I certainly didn't have much responsibility (no family, girlfriend, kids). I hadn't gotten much sleep the night before and was catching an unnecessarily early flight back home to the city. I closed my eyes, covered them with a pair of eye shades,

and dozed off. Everything seemed normal. I had no idea that when I would wake up in only two short hours, my life would be forever changed.

When the wheels of the plane slammed into the ground and jolted me awake, I felt even worse. I was completely out of it, like when you're awoken in the middle of the night and momentarily have no idea where you are, only this wasn't momentary. Slowly, I removed my shades and glanced at my watch to check the time. Interestingly, I couldn't make out what I saw. It was very blurry. *Hmm, my eyes must still be adjusting,* I thought. *Let me just give it another minute or so.* I rubbed my eyes and tried again. Still bad.

I was beginning to realize the magnitude of the issue. My left eye was completely blurry, almost to the point of no light being allowed in. It was painful even to move my eyes or look in a different direction, as if some muscle inside my eye were being pulled tight every time. Something was definitely wrong. But what the hell could have happened while I was asleep? Did someone knock me in the eye with the beverage cart? Did I develop pinkeye? Did I fall? Frantically, my mind scrolled through the possibilities. Disembarking the plane, I tried my best with one working eye to navigate the frightening new world around me. There were walls and railings I'd never really paid much attention to now bouncing me around like a ball in a pinball machine. My heart started racing—I tried to stifle the panic and focus solely on getting home as quickly as possible. Maybe by then things would be better?

The two senses you *really* don't want to mess with are your vision and hearing. It can be very scary if things change for only a few seconds or minutes. I didn't want to create drama over a minor thing, so I decided to give it a day to get better before acting upon it. Thankfully, I made it home in one piece. I chose to sleep it off, falling deep into blissfully ignorant dreams.

I woke up the next morning with the same loss of vision and distinct pain in my left eye. Okay, now it was time to panic. I immediately called an eye specialist and asked to be seen as soon as possible. To my relief, they were able to see me that afternoon. The doctor peered into my eye and started asking questions, one of which was very peculiar: "Were you near a cat at all during the weekend?" What the hell would a cat have to do with my eye being damaged? Scratching me? I tried to think . . . in fact, yes, I remembered my friend having a cat where I stayed.

"Yes," I said, "there was a cat."

"Mhm," he said in that ambiguous doctor tone.

He suggested I get blood work done. He had a sheet with a checklist of the world's worst diseases: AIDS/HIV, hepatitis, cancer, Lyme disease, and toxoplasmosis, among many others.

After an hour or so, the results were in, and it was confirmed: I had toxoplasmosis. He immediately prescribed me a trifecta of incredibly powerful steroids, both oral medications and eye drops.

"Doc," I said nervously, "what the hell *is* toxoplasmosis?"

"Toxoplasmosis is a parasite," he explained. He wasn't looking right at me. He seemed . . . concerned. "You can never kill it, but you can put it in a dormant state. The gut of a cat often serves as a host, usually picked up from killing a mouse. The parasite sheds millions of oocysts, active parasites, through its feces, which in turn can be easily delivered to a human. That's why they tell pregnant women to stay away from kitty litter—it can be lethal to an unborn fetus."

I stared at him, disgusted and morbidly terrified. I was being told that I had an incurable disease? I thought about what he was saying. In other words, a cat eats a mouse that is carrying the parasite. The cat shits in the kitty litter and steps on the shit, which is now on the cat's feet. Now, everywhere the cat goes and everything it touches has microscopic parasites on it that are highly contagious. Let's say the cat jumps on your bed. Maybe you touch your sheets or comforter and get into bed. Maybe you bite your nails. Maybe you eat some food and lick some ketchup off your finger. Or maybe you sleep on your side and put your mouth on the pillowcase where the cat stepped. Boom. Without realizing it, you just ingested a parasite that cannot be killed.

The good news is that 95 percent of people are healthy and their immune system will keep the parasite in check. Who are the people at risk, generally? 1) Immunocompromised patients undergoing chemo or radiation treatments, 2) pregnant women, 3) those who eat raw or undercooked meat—often hunters who eat venison. There is another way of contracting this disease called congenital, meaning it was passed to you from your parents through birth, but was lying dormant until just the right time.

In a small percentage of patients who do contract the parasite (the lucky few!), it travels through the bloodstream directly into the vulnerable eye cells, which is called "ocular toxoplasmosis." This causes inflammation inside the eye (intraocular inflammation) not visible from the outside. Here's the kicker: It's not the parasite itself that causes any damage to the eye. It's the body's immune response and inflammation to the parasite that causes permanent damage and scarring on the retina (retinal pigmentosa, or loss of pigment on the retina).

The statistics on 'toxo' are pretty mind-boggling. According to the CDC, nearly 40 million Americans are currently infected with the parasite (Toxoplasma gondii), with an additional 200,000+ new cases each year. That's roughly 11 percent of the U.S. population. It's also the leading cause of death in foodborne illness. But 95 percent of those infected have no idea and will never experience any symptoms.

You know how else you can have a weakened immune system? By

partying in Miami for three days straight, drinking excessively, and not sleeping. But if you think about the situation, it was a comedy of errors. Everything had to align perfectly in order to create the right environment for me to contract the parasite. 1) I had to have a weakened immune system by partying too much (not too difficult), 2) I had to stay in a house with a cat (not uncommon, but not every household has one), 3) that cat had to be actively shedding the parasite's oocysts with a new infection, usually within two weeks of eating a mouse (rare), and 4) I had to be the unlucky one whose eye got attacked (very rare).

So, why do I tell you all this? What's the point? First off, it's interesting to learn about, right? Second, there are so many crazy diseases and things you haven't heard of that amply exist in the world (brain-eating amoebas from lake water?), yet that have such low public awareness. But third, and the most important lesson of all, is that your health can change on a dime. Literally, in a split second.

The reality is that we're so lucky to be alive. Every moment. Every day. There are so many people who died too soon and should be here with us right now but aren't. Life is short—your health can change in the blink of an infected eye. For me, it's made me appreciate life that much more. I know this sounds cliché, but every day you're breathing is a great day. Especially in a place like New York City, where you can easily lose perspective of the bigger picture and get caught up in your own little world, it's important to remind yourself of this.

With that said, should we be completely risk-averse, living in a padded room our entire life? Of course not! You need to live your life. Go outside, party, have fun, but do so with some degree of caution. The reality is I could get hit by a bus tomorrow just stepping onto the street, but this doesn't mean I shouldn't ever cross the street again. No one is immune to everything. We need to focus on the things within our control and simply embrace those that are not. Should I continually live in fear that this parasite could reawaken in my eye and cause further damage? Unfortunately, this possibility is out of my control. All I can do is try to live a healthy lifestyle, take care of my body and mind, and, hopefully, it won't be an issue.

A couple of real-life lessons: If you experience a change in vision, time is of the essence. Don't wait. You need to be put on medicine or steroids as soon as possible. There is no trophy for being macho. Also, try not to freak out. This can be hard. Your mind will start spinning, rabbit-holing deeper and deeper into a darkening abyss. Things will get better, I can assure you. But it's torturous waiting . . . I get it. Our brains are pretty powerful devices—they can fill in the blanks with terrifying ideas. It's okay to take risks in life. Just make sure they're calculated, not reckless.

TINNITUS

Shortly after my eye problems emerged, I acquired tinnitus, also a result of partying too much (although with tinnitus there is a cumulative aspect that takes place over years). While I was fortunate not to suffer any actual hearing loss, I was left with a residual "ringing" in both ears as a byproduct. Thankfully it's become tolerable, but it led me through a very dark period of my life, where I thought I wasn't going to be able to live through it—I didn't want to. I briefly had scary suicidal thoughts. But I think it's important to raise some awareness for those suffering every day from this nasty, incurable phantom sound.

Have you ever been to a rock concert, or a party with loud music blasting over the speakers, and heard a loud ringing noise in your ears immediately after you left? Now imagine if that loud ringing noise never went away and was playing in the background as a soundtrack for the rest of your life. Welcome to my world.

Every time you hear ringing, whether you realize it or not, you are doing damage to your ears. In other words, you should never hear ringing. *Ever.* If you are, then that environment is too loud. Fortunately, for most people this ringing noise is temporary and fades away completely over the next few hours. However, we're not machines, and everyone's ears have a threshold; a breaking point. This damage from loud noise accumulates over time to a point where your ears become permanently damaged. There is no known cure or even solid scientific understanding as to why this occurs; there are several different theories, originating with damaged cilia (tiny hair-like structures deep inside your ear that some animals can regenerate but humans cannot), heightened neurotoxicity, and NMDA receptor antagonists/beta blockers, to name a few.

Throughout high school and college, I attended many music concerts. However, it was one weekend in Miami when I went to nightclubs for three consecutive nights that did me over. I didn't give my ears time to recover and reset. One of the nightclubs was blowing an airhorn (yes, an AIRHORN) over the already incredibly loud music. I've never heard noise that loud in my life, to be honest . . . it must have approached 140+ decibels. It's easy to say, "Well, Peter, that was irresponsible behavior," and I may agree with you. But I don't think I should be permanently punished for wanting to have fun with friends. My poor decision-making doesn't give nightclub owners license to damage my hearing. Ironic, too, that I'm a paying customer for this "fun." If you hurt all your customers, you won't have any left! But I digress.

Over the last few years, I've become a human guinea pig, investing a lot of time, money, and mental energy in experimental therapies, some of which helped, and some of which didn't. I travelled to Vienna, Austria, for a non-FDA-approved IV drug named Tinnitin (caroverine hydrochloride). This initially made my tinnitus louder, but over time it quieted down. I flew down to a clinic in North Carolina that was participating in an experimental trial for a drug called AM-101 (manufactured by Auris Medical, which is basically a variation of esketamine, or the recreational drug "Special K"). I opted out at the last minute in fear of receiving a placebo (since double-blind studies won't reveal whether you're actually getting the medication or not) and received intratympanic (inside the eardrum by making a small incision) steroid injections. This helped immensely, even if it didn't cure it.

Given the subjective nature of this condition, it's very hard to diagnose, and even more difficult to understand or sympathize with. There is an extremely fine line, psychologically, between "tolerable" noise and "intolerable" noise on any given day. I feel fortunate that for me, personally, the sounds of the outside world mask the background tinnitus so I don't notice it 95 percent of my day. The only time it really becomes a problem is in extremely quiet surroundings with no sounds from nature, or at night when I lay my head on a pillow, covering one of my ears and thus creating a noise vacuum. For this reason, I must always sleep with a white noise machine (or, for millennials, an iPhone app). The most depressing thought is that I'll never be able to enjoy pure silence again. However, even today there are brief moments when I don't even notice it, and it feels like actual silence. I cherish those moments very much, even if they last only a few seconds.

Okay, enough from Debbie Downer. What does this all *mean*? And what is the solution? I've had a lot of time (several years, in fact) to think about this topic. A few thoughts: we created this condition. It is man-made in the sense that other than lightning strikes or physiological birth defects, there's nothing on planet Earth naturally capable of producing sound so loud that it would damage your hearing. With the advancement of speaker technology, we're capable of producing louder and louder noise (old speakers weren't even capable of handling such high wattage; they would literally "blow").

Add increased headphone use to the mix, and you have an entire upcoming generation of young people who are going to have tinnitus and/or hearing loss (you can have one without the other). If you look at many of the new tinnitus cases, it's a whole lot of young, affluent kids getting damaged from nightclubs, or even spin classes like SoulCycle. I know this because I scour the chat forums online about tinnitus and read distressed posts from young people. This is quite a contrast, historically speaking. It used to be primarily war veterans who would acquire tinnitus from grenade blasts or other loud weaponry; now it's fitness enthusiasts going to spinning classes. I think prevention will only occur with 1) increased public awareness and education, especially targeted to people under thirty and 2) government action. For example, you know how every coffee cup says,

"WARNING: HOT COFFEE" on it? I think there should be a small warning sign on the door before you enter any nightclub that says, "WARNING: THE ENVIRONMENT YOU ARE ABOUT TO ENTER IS DANGEROUSLY LOUD. WE RECOMMEND USING EARPLUGS." And the venue should be required, upon a patron request, to provide cheap foam earplugs (don't worry, they cost like two pennies to make).

Did you know there are existing laws on outdoor decibel volume but not on indoor noise? You can make an indoor room as loud as you want, even dangerous/torture-like, and it's not illegal or subject to a fine for commercial establishments. There's a lot of social stigma against wearing earplugs, especially among immature people in their early twenties. "What are you, a grandpa? Why do you need earplugs?"

They look ugly and weird. It can be embarrassing. No one wants to have to explain themselves or feel different from their friends, especially at that age. I understand what that feels like. Even though you're being smart and protecting yourself, other kids don't understand. The social pressures become too great, which is why many younger people at risk don't wear earplugs. I want to start a social campaign with TV ads that makes it look cool to be smart and wear earplugs when going out at night. I'd also like to start a company that makes aesthetically appealing earplugs for kids, teens, and young people in general, like a fashion trend. There would be different styles and patterns that make people actually *want* to use them. The more they do, the safer their ears become.

In the meantime, go to a hearing doctor (otolaryngologist) and book an appointment to get some custom "sleeper plugs" made. They're about $100 a pair and will be the greatest investment you'll ever make. It will save you thousands of hours and dollars in further hearing treatments and anxieties down the road. They're extremely low-profile, flush in the ear, and see-through so no one can notice. I don't leave home without mine, ever. In today's noisy world, you never know when you'll need them.

05

That Time
I Was Vegan

ISTARTED BECOMING VERY HEALTH-CONSCIOUS WHILE AN
UNDERGRADUATE AT THE UNIVERSITY OF MIAMI. Everyone
seemed to be in ridiculously good shape. But it wasn't until
both my parents were diagnosed with cancer that I got very
serious about nutrition. After I watched the documentary
Forks Over Knives, I had determined it was time to go vegan.
I was full-on vegan for two years, between 2012 and 2014,
before deciding to stop. People often ask me, "What was that
experience like?" This is my answer.

After the fallout from my parents' dual cancer diagnoses, I started
researching the genetic and epigenetic roots of disease—the ways in which
our DNA is coded and how environment and lifestyle choices trigger the
expression of certain genes. What I read about diet and nutrition made a
huge impact on me, and though our family doctors told me my parents'
cancers weren't genetic, I decided to take action. I lost twenty-five pounds
by adopting a vegan diet, which I maintained for two years, as well as
eliminating carbs, sugar, and oils. I became deeply passionate about clean
food, and very aware of how easily people sabotage their own attempts at
healthy eating. Though I didn't remain vegan, I love sharing with others the
insights into better health that I gained during this era of my life.

There are two types of vegans: 1) *Moral Vegans*—these are the more
commonly stereotyped and mocked individuals, who can sometimes be

incredibly outspoken or outlandish to get their point across (think PETA animal rights groups throwing paint on fur, going naked, etc.), and 2) *Health Vegans*—these folks are driven primarily for personal health benefits. While they're supportive of greater political causes (saving animals and saving the planet), they tend to be more reserved and less divisive on these issues. So, if you meet someone who claims to be vegan, it's important to first ask them, "Are you doing it for moral or health reasons?" Depending on their answer, you'll be able to assess how strongly they feel on the subject and how vociferous they're going to be if you make any comments on it. (Pro tip: don't try to get in a discussion or challenge a moral vegan. You are NOT going to make them think any differently, and it will quickly turn into a heated argument.)

Personally, I was really only doing it for health reasons. I read a lot about the harmful effects that animal protein and animal byproducts have on the human body and was/still am convinced about it. I apologize in advance if I sound preachy. I really try to refrain from judging others or telling people how they should live their life, but I do feel strongly that one of the worst things you can put in your body is milk (other than human milk). One of the leading researchers on milk protein (casein, caseinate to be exact), Dr. T. Colin Campbell, has shown many direct links between cancer growth and casein. In short, he was able to "turn on and turn off" cancer cells (see more in *The China Study*). I'll give my brief spiel on milk, then forever hold my peace.

"But you gotta have milk! It gives you calcium, and strong bones!" Well, we can't say marketing and advertising doesn't work. Remember all of those "Got Milk?" campaigns, funded by the dairy industry and lobbying groups? The reality is that Americans consume some of the highest amounts of milk per capita than most other countries in the world, yet we also have one of the highest incidences of bone fractures. If we're drinking all this milk, shouldn't we have super strong Superman bones to go with it? Obviously, there could be a million reasons for this disparity. But let's consider some other facts about humans and milk and use some common sense.

It all seems very unnatural, if you ask me. We are the *only* species that drinks another species' milk. We are the *only* species that drinks milk after breastfeeding and throughout our life. Think about this; what is cow milk intended to do? It's intended to turn a baby calf into a full-blown cow within a matter of only two years! Think of the size difference between these life stages. Every time you drink milk, you're pumping all those growth hormones into your small human body. There's a reason why Muscle Milk and all those other workout shakes contain casein.

If there's only one thing I would advise anyone to do, *please* remove dairy from your diet. It may actually save your life. The most frustrating part is that most people, especially cancer victims, don't start implementing these changes until they've been diagnosed and it's too late. I firmly believe there is a compounded, cumulative, and preventative effect of stopping dairy intake *now,* while you're young, that will pay great dividends later in life. But trying to get millennials (or most people, for that matter) to think more than five days ahead in their super-plugged-in lives is an almost impossible task.

When people hear the word "vegan," they also commonly mistake that with being "healthy." As any actual vegan will tell you, this is not an accurate association (restaurants in particular love to use this branding). You can eat potato chips all day long and still call yourself a vegan. Also, I would argue it's much more difficult to lose weight going vegan; it can often be a very high-carb diet, and people rely on lots of sauces and oils for added flavor, all of which are calorie-heavy. The "healthy vegan" association assumes that the individual is constantly eating a whole, all-natural, and unprocessed diet. Yes, if you're only eating vegetables all day long with no oils, spreads, or sauces, then you could lose weight. But this is rarely the case.

My experience going vegan was a difficult one, at least initially. I experienced a major dip in energy. It's important, especially at first, to constantly be eating nuts, beans, or legumes as a source of protein. If not, you'll feel very lethargic and constantly low on energy; it can be a big adjustment if you stop eating meat cold turkey (no pun intended). Once you get over this initial bump, you should be just fine. But it can be a frustrating and emotionally draining process. Another suggestion would be to slowly wean yourself off of meat instead.

After two years of being a vegan, I stopped. To be honest, I missed the taste of some foods too much. But more importantly, I was having difficulty reaching the physical goals I'd set for myself in the gym. It's very hard (but not impossible) to recreate the leanness of turkey or chicken nutritionally (although many are trying with new vegan meat substitute products). I would work out constantly and still not be able to push myself as hard as I wanted to. I would often hit a wall while exercising, a point of no return where I knew that was the most I could do that day. At that point, I decided it was time to give up being a vegan. I eat meat, but I still firmly believe it's causing deleterious effects on my internal body. I just try to limit my intake and focus on why I'm doing it. Life is full of choices, and you have to choose your battles carefully. I choose meat poison over milk poison. But that's my choice, and I respect the ones that others make.

06

The Power of Positivity

EVEN WHEN I OWNED A HEALTHY, FARM-TO-TABLE **RESTAURANT, I WASN'T BEING HEALTHY.** I was overeating from stress, not sleeping enough, and generally miserable. Eventually, a friend brought me to a meditation class, and I fell in love. Over the course of the last two years, I've become passionate about health and wellness, yoga, meditation, healthy eating, and fitness. I've learned that everything is connected, and positivity is contagious. I'm here to share that power with you.

New Yorkers are constantly bombarded with stimuli. Taxi cabs, billboards, construction, you name it. There's so much going on around us all the time that our minds become exhausted without us even realizing it. Also, I think New Yorkers like to stress each other out for no reason. I'm serious; it's a phenomenon. It's a very competitive city in which many people are overly concerned with status and are therefore judgmental of other people. It's easy to lose perspective on the bigger picture. For this reason, I think it's important to force yourself to take a ten-minute break in the middle of the day, calm your mind, and proceed.

Meditation allows me to do this. It brings emotions to the surface and provides clarity. More importantly, meditation allows me to stay calm and not get overly excited by external stimuli. The point of meditation is not to "clear your mind," but to focus on your breathing and allow the mind to

naturally wander. Thoughts act like clouds in the sky and will silently drift by. The goal is to simply observe your emotional reaction with these thoughts from a safe distance, without getting "caught in the weeds" of them and, if/when this naturally occurs, to return to your breath. I highly recommend that you try it. For me, it has been life-changing.

I believe that when one lives in constant positivity, they're in a state of flow. Magical things can happen when you adopt this mindset. Huge pieces fall into place seemingly by chance. You get that promotion you've been looking for. You stumble upon your dream house by accident and the price is right. You get a free upgrade at the hotel you're staying at—whatever the case may be, it feels like a doorway has opened up to you, and life becomes rife with endless possibilities.

However, the same goes when one lives in a constant state of negativity, worry, and fear. When you're in this mindset, you'll notice that when something "bad" happens to you at the beginning of the day (let's say you stubbed your toe), things start spiraling out of control. Not the moment you stubbed your toe, but the moment you thought, "Well, well, well. I guess I know how today is going to be."

In that split second, you have cursed your entire day. The moment you *thought* it, the universe sprang into action to craft that reality for you. For example, afterward you may have gone into your car and gotten your coat stuck in the door, tearing it because you were too impatient to simply open the door. (Again!) Then you got your coffee in the drive-thru but on your way into work you noticed the cashier overcharged you. (Again!) You walked through the rain because you forgot your umbrella in the frustration that erupted after you stubbed your toe. Once you get inside your office building, you start sniffling from the cold. Someone notices. "Hey, you okay?"

You hesitate. *How could they know? Is it really that obvious?*

"Uh, yeah," you say. "Why?"

They raise an eyebrow. "You don't look so good. You look like you're coming down with something."

(Again!)

For the next few hours you focus on that statement with such fervor that you bring it into being. You sneeze a couple times, then feel lightheaded. Finally, you ask to go home early, where you languish in bed and curse the few hours and dollars you missed due to this stupid cold.

See? It's a spiral. An unnecessary spiral, at that, and this way of thinking can make your life miserable, forever. But let's paint a different scenario. You get out of bed, stub your toe. *Ouch!* That hurt. But you look down. No bruising or bleeding. *No biggie.* You shake it off and have a nice, relaxing shower. After breakfast you grab your coat and umbrella. You're relaxed, and your movements are graceful, so you don't catch your coat in the car door. Then you grab your coffee in the drive-thru, but you notice while you're walking into work that they overcharged you—one dollar. *Maybe I'll bring them the receipt and get a free cup of coffee next time.*

Inside your work, you're warm, focused, and productive. Your boss takes notice and commends you, says something positive like, "If you keep this up, you'll be in your own office someday." Maybe he's just trying to be nice, but hey, it *is* nice, isn't it? And if you stay within this state of flow, his words will come true, if you will them.

In a nutshell, this is the stark difference between positivity and negativity, between a life of fullness and a life of emptiness. It all starts within one place: Your mind. Your thoughts. Think well and be well—it's that simple.

If you want to change your surroundings, then the power is within you at all times to do so. If you want to change from within, the same goes. I fundamentally disagree with the statement, "People don't change." I'm living proof that people can change. We all have the power to change ourselves, we just have to *want* it. I've said this before, and I'll repeat it: It's the journey, not the destination. Focus on just one goal at a time, one step at a time. Worry about today *today* and tomorrow *tomorrow*. Better yet, don't worry at all! It's great to have a plan, but just know that life and health can change so fast. Make intentional decisions, not aimless ones. Focus on being the best person you can be, for yourself and your friends. And above all, love yourself. You cannot love others if you don't first love yourself.

At the end of the day, for me, happiness is the most important thing. You cannot pay me to be miserable—I don't care how much you're paying. People want to be around other positive, supportive people. Remember, positivity is infectious. Share it and embrace it, and you will flourish.

Weal

True wealth isn't just having loads of cash and possessions—in fact, material riches can sometimes be more of a hindrance than a blessing

thy Millennial

07

Party Like Jay Gatsby

IN COLLEGE I THREW MASSIVE, OPULENT BIRTHDAY PARTIES FOR MYSELF—THE BENEFICIARIES WERE AROUND 400 OF MY CLOSEST FRIENDS. From renting out entire nightclubs to reserving swanky hotel rooftop penthouses, I created unique, festive spaces for my friends and classmates to have memorable experiences. The first party was for my twenty-first birthday, which happened to coincide with the time of my parents' divorce. They were feeling overly generous, and I channeled that generosity to my college campus. The parties continued for five years in a row—to this day, University of Miami alumni remember these events. In many ways, these lavish experiences were the ways I used my wealth and privilege to craft an identity apart from the very people from whom I had inherited this same wealth.

I advertised the party on Facebook as "The Biggest Birthday Party U.M. has ever seen." The concept was simple: leave your wallet at home. I'm not really sure where the idea originated from. It was in part ego-driven, and I also just wanted to make an impact on campus. It was only supposed to be a one-time thing. My twenty-first birthday lined up perfectly with the return of students from summer break. That's right. I rented out an affordable

nightclub in downtown Miami with no cover charge (granted it was a Monday night, when they would usually be closed, so it was a favorable and heavily discounted negotiation). I arranged for free buses to shuttle students to and from campus all night, and I planned for an open bar. All you had to do was show up, and the rest was taken care of.

I know this all sounds crazy expensive. Don't get me wrong; it wasn't cheap. But a Monday night in Miami in the middle of summer isn't as crazy as some of my New York readers might think. If you're smart about it, you can do it on a budget. I didn't start getting nervous until approximately 500 people showed up by the Panhellenic building on campus to get on the buses. I thought the campus police would surely shut it down and I'd get a call from the dean of students the next morning. Or even worse, they would write about it in the school newspaper. But everything went off smoothly. The buses were shuttling people back and forth to the nightclub, and everyone got in without trouble. People were dancing on top of tables and bars. Everywhere I turned my head, people were making out with each other. It was wild! Walking around campus the next day, everyone was talking about it . . . about *me*. I felt like a king; it was the greatest high I'd ever experienced. I'll never forget thinking, *I just had 5 percent of the entire University of Miami undergraduates at my birthday party last night*.

I probably should have stopped after the one party. But the reverberation felt from that night was so potent and impactful that as another year passed, I felt obligated to do something again. I felt unnecessary pressure from my peers; I had a reputation to uphold! "Peter Darrow birthday parties" became its own brand, so I decided to keep the annual bash going. Every year was a little different; one year I rented a party boat to cruise around Miami for the evening; another year I rented the rooftop penthouse of the Shore Club Hotel (which ultimately got broken up because some drunk idiot was chucking beer bottles off the roof – thankfully no one was hurt), and the final event was a South Beach mansion I rented for the night. Each party averaged about 300–400 people and got more sophisticated every year, with custom, unique party favors like shot glasses designed with the silhouettes of naked girls and palm trees. By the time it was all said and done, I could have easily become a professional party planner. I had more experience than most people starting out in the business. I seriously considered it. But, ultimately, I decided I was destined to achieve much bigger things.

Does this all make me sound a bit overprivileged? Perhaps. I try to always be mindful of that. But people are still going to judge. One way to view all this is that I was extremely generous and decided to share these experiences with my friends (and all their friends.) I think when you're in a position of wealth of any kind, be it financial, spiritual or otherwise, it's best when shared. I could have spent my birthdays with cocaine, prostitutes, and lavish dinners, but I preferred to spend it with the people I cared about in ways that made us all happy. The bigger their smiles, the better I felt. In this way, my birthdays weren't just about *me*—they were about all of us coming together to share a nice time.

I could have easily not written about this—it can be a bit embarrassing. But I don't shy away from my past decisions. I think this fun phase of my life is worth embracing and, at worst, it makes for a good conversation starter and some wild memories. So, don't bother asking me if I regret it. I don't.

08

Darrow's Farm Fresh

MY FATHER ALWAYS TOLD ME, "YOU'LL ONLY BE SUCCESSFUL AT THINGS YOU'RE PASSIONATE ABOUT." One of the things I'm very passionate about is helping people through food and healthier living. After my father passed away, I decided to follow my dream to own a healthy, farm-to-table restaurant in Manhattan. "Darrow's Farm Fresh Takeout" (we later dropped the "takeout") opened on January 26, 2015, near Union Square. It was a beautiful and behemoth space, at approximately 5,600 square feet, with a total staff of twenty-five. We were in operation for about a year before deciding to close. Although the business was short-lived, I had an amazing journey, and I'm proud of what I built. I also learned an incredible amount about myself, and other people, in the process.

SOUTHAMPTON, NEW YORK
SATURDAY, JUNE 20, 2015, 8:30 A.M.

My girlfriend and I desperately needed some romantic time together. We'd both been working non-stop the last four weeks without any break, and we'd barely seen each other. It was straining our relationship, to say the least. So, I

decided to rent a cottage for the weekend and have a relaxing time together outside of the hustle and bustle of New York. However, due to (*surprise!*) work, we were delayed in leaving and didn't arrive in Long Island until late in the evening Friday. I woke up the next morning to a phone call—it was my head chef.

"Bobby! What's going on?" I asked, trying to sound chipper even though work was the last thing I wanted to be dealing with on my long-awaited break. I will never forget his words.

"Pete," he said. "We have a flood."

My heart sank. Great, more work. "Like a leak? Where?"

"No, not a leak," he said. "The entire second floor dining room is *flooded with water.*"

I thought about that a moment. Still, my mind hadn't processed the full fuckery of it.

"Flooded?" I repeated. "Well . . . can we get the team together fast to clean it up?"

"That's not even the problem. It's started to seep through the floor into the kitchen below. I don't think we're going to be able to open today."

There was a long beat of silence, during which I began to grow nauseous.

"How many brunch reservations do we have?" I asked quietly. I didn't want to know the answer.

"A hundred and fifty."

"Fuck."

"Yep," he agreed. We were silent a moment as I considered my options. "Pete, to be honest, I don't think you'll be opening for a while. And I don't think I want to stay in this environment."

I squeezed the bridge of my nose between my fingers, closing my eyes tightly. "Bobby, don't quit on me right now, please. Just hang on for a few hours and we'll discuss it in person. I'm coming back right now. I'll be there in two hours."

I turned slowly to face my girlfriend. Her face had fallen—she knew this trip would not be continuing. Because of me.

How was I supposed to be prepared for this type of situation? They didn't teach me this in business school. What's the script? Where's the playbook for a major flood and disappointing the love of your life? I felt way in over my head. While my girlfriend was supportive, she was obviously upset (as was I). I had never felt more alone in my entire life. I was on an island somewhere in the Pacific Ocean by myself. I was the boss. I was the guy who had to fix everything, but I didn't even know where to start. Everyone relied on me for an answer. The pissed-off staff. My head chef. The angry patrons. Some infinitesimal mechanism of the universe had malfunctioned and sprung a leak (literally) that seemed to wash away my dream in a single day. And no one was there to help me through it. No one to say, "Hey, Pete, I know it's not your fault, it just sucks, man. What can we do?" There was a revolting sense of doom permeating the place when I got back. It was on everyone's faces, and the look in their eyes gave me the impression that I had caused the damn flood myself.

Not only was my entire staff not going to be able to work or get paid, but I also had 150+ upset brunch guests to personally deal with, as well as another 200+ booked for Sunday, our busiest meal of the week. Well, not anymore.

I wanted to crawl up in a hole somewhere and cry. I just wanted a little sympathy from someone. But instead, I was the most hated person in that moment, for something that was beyond my control. I'll never forget that sense of powerlessness. So often when you're the leader of a business, if something goes wrong, it's your ass.

I wanted to quit, too. But I couldn't. After that episode, we were closed for almost a full week (an eternity in the cash-flow-dependent restaurant business). They had to rip off part of the second floor and fumigate the entire area for any mold. Fortunately, we had insurance to cover it. But insurance can't reimburse reputational damage or customer goodwill, which was more damaged than the building itself.

I can say with confidence that of all business types, restaurants are the most difficult and the most stressful. Restaurant owners deal with a million different variables: catering, marketing and promotions, special events, staffing, payroll, purveyors and vendors, advertising, Yelp reviews, the wrong music or ambiance, air conditioning issues, poor lighting, food allergies, cleanliness, homeless people walking in off the street . . . you name it. Yes, I had a general manager to help me. But I was doing 80 percent of the work myself. And I was overwhelmed.

The people who work in the restaurant industry are different from those who work in other industries. For starters, it's not a career for most people. Most workers do it part-time or just temporarily between life stages to make a little extra cash, since restaurants generally under-pay employees for their hard work due to extreme fixed costs such as rising Manhattan rents (blame greedy landlords) and other industry costs. Plus, it's a very cash-heavy business, mostly tip-based. As a result of these factors, restaurant staff are generally not the most motivated talent pool. Employee turnover is high and the barriers of switching jobs are low. Job availability increases or decreases proportionally to how busy or slow the restaurant is. So, getting the "right" staffing is a never-ending challenge for any owner.

Interestingly enough, alcoholism plagues the restaurant industry. I blame high-stress demands placed on management, long working hours, and constantly dealing with unruly customers. It's also not an industry that values education. No one gives a shit if you have a fancy MBA. It's not going

to open any doors for you—in fact, it actually may hurt you. Given that the workforce is generally less educated, having an advanced degree may serve to further isolate you from your staff. Yes, it's good to know stuff in order to run a business efficiently. But the restaurant industry is experience-based. You want to employ the kind of people who grew up in a kitchen, working in their family restaurant all their life. That's why many chefs become restaurant-owners themselves. Because if the shit hits the fan and everybody quits, they can retrain and rehire quickly and run the show themselves.

I also saw a ton of employees lying, stealing, and not showing up to work. This is due mostly to hourly employees who work very hard, but, again, aren't loyal. They often fail to see the big picture that if the business does well, then they will also do well. But the harsh reality is this: How can you think long-term when you're living day-to-day, paycheck-to-paycheck, to get by? Of course they're stealing. They need the money to live and you're not providing it, which may not even be your fault. The restaurant business is a Catch-22.

Finally, there are a lot of dirty and tough purveyors and vendors in this industry. While it may not be as mafia-infested as it once was, food purveyors are constantly raising prices (in tiny increments so you don't notice) without telling you. Before you know it, you have ridiculously expensive invoices. And guess what? If you refuse to pay, or if you challenge it, they simply won't deliver anything to you. Then you can't serve it to customers, and they'll complain and hurt your business. So, you're screwed either way.

"What motivated you to open a restaurant?" It's an excellent question, and one to which I'm still trying to figure out the answer. When my parents were both diagnosed with cancer, I became hyperaware of what I was putting into my body. It was soon thereafter that I became vegan. But as I addressed previously, I quickly discovered that eating vegan did not necessarily ensure a healthy diet. There were too many oils and heavy sauces. And I felt treated like some alien species by my own friends and family. Any time we'd go out to dinner, it always became a huge production. "What can *Peter* eat? What's on the menu? Oh, no, we can't go there. He's *vegan*."

While we're back on the topic, let me clear up a common misperception: the cuisine of the restaurant has absolutely nothing to do with whether a vegan can go there. There are steak houses with steamed vegetables, and there are Mediterranean places that use butter on every menu item. Even in a place as big as New York City with thousands of restaurants, you would be surprised how few are actually "healthy" (meaning not adding a ton of salt, cream, sugar, heavy oils, sauces, butter, etc.).

This was extremely frustrating to me. Why can't cats and dogs live together, figuratively speaking? You should be able to go out anywhere without having to constantly worry if your friend or significant other can eat there. I decided I was going to solve this problem and create a space where both meat-eaters and non-meat-eaters could come together. Our mission at Darrow's Farm Fresh was to serve clean, light, unprocessed, and (when possible) organic. No cooking with fryers. No butter. Only light, healthy oils. Everything would be labeled on the menu as gluten-free, vegan, etc. In fact, I don't even like the word "vegan." It's generationally misunderstood; we used "plant-based" instead.

Because we were focused on healthy food, we catered to a lot of clientele within that industry. Thus, we were able to create strategic partnerships with major health and fitness brands and local studios. This is one of the accomplishments I'm most proud of. Within only a few short months, we'd partnered with Nike, Lululemon, SoulCycle, Equinox, Exhale, Reebok, Uber Eats, Athleta, Tonehouse, Bandier, Fhitting Room, and NY Health and Racquet Club, among others. This could comprise different things, including cross-promotional marketing, giveaways, hosting special events for VIP customers, emails, free meals, free classes, discounts, newsletters, custom private label cold-pressed juices, etc. How did I do this so quickly? Sheer hard work and determination. No previous connections. Just walking into places and, introducing myself. Business is built on relationships. I was working nearly 100 hours a week, but never in my wildest dreams did I imagine I would be able to partner with some of these awesome brands. That made it all worth it.

Conversely, serving healthy food has downsides, the biggest one being that customers are very vocal and passionate about their food, and, accordingly, they are painfully aware of every mistake you make. While I appreciate their loyalty and trust in our brand, it can become overwhelming. For example, if I own a burrito joint and went a little light on the sour cream, someone may say something. If I own a healthy restaurant and forget the walnuts on a kale salad, it's the apocalypse. Immediate bashing and one-star Yelp reviews. Not only is the customer upset, but they also want to sabotage your business publicly and burn it down.

Of course, not all customers are like this. There are some who express real appreciation and gratitude. But the reality is that most people (intentionally or not) only express themselves to complain. This was the most emotionally draining part for me. Yes, you are a paying customer and have a right to be upset. But so often I wished I could say, "If you only knew what I've personally sacrificed in terms of money, time away from loved ones, and stress in an attempt to provide you with healthier food options. I'm trying to help you, and in five seconds you're squashing my hopes and dreams!"

What I learned is that when people are paying for something, all their other personality traits go out the door. The nicest person in the world can suddenly become very mean. But paying doesn't give you the right to treat other people like dirt. It's also amazing to me how often people want things for free, even if you make a minor mistake. "You left out the napkins. I want this meal comped." Or, "The side of spinach was cold when it arrived. I want it free."

In hospitality, there's no hiding behind the screen and emailing your response to a complaint. The customer is right there, in your face. You have to learn how to delicately and diplomatically de-escalate the situation with 100 other customers watching. Not only are you risking losing one customer, but, depending on how you handle it, you might lose some of the other 100 as well.

I'll leave you with one last story, both sad and comical. We'd been open less than a month and were finally picking up steam. The 12:30 lunch crowd was catching onto us. One day, for the first time, we were slammed. We had a line to the door, and it was all hands on deck. All of a sudden, the smoothie blender stopped working. *Weird*, I thought. I pulled the cord out of the socket and put it into a different one; it started working again. Crisis diverted.

Every employee, myself included, was busy serving customers. Thirty seconds passed, and the blender cut out again. Was there something wrong with the socket? Then suddenly the POS (point of sale) system shut down. The POS system is what you depend on to make sales transactions. It's the machine needed to pay with credit cards, cash, anything. Frantic, I rushed downstairs to the basement and asked the prep cooks, "What the hell is going on?"

"I don't know. Some of the equipment stopped working."

My head was spinning as I tried to brainstorm every possible idea to fix this problem. I had 100+ customers upstairs depending on a solution. "It's got to be electrical! Let me check the circuit breaker panel." I ran to the circuit panel and opened it. Low and behold, several of the breakers were flipped to the off position. I switched them back on. Voila! Everything started working again. I was clammy with sweat. But then . . ."Oh, no."

Within ten seconds, several of the switches flipped back off. Something must have been wired badly. We were using too much power, and I didn't have the time to go to every socket to determine which one was causing the problem. I didn't even have time to run back upstairs and let my staff know what the hell was going on. I had to do whatever I could in that moment to survive the next thirty minutes of lunch.

There's only one thing I can do, I determined.

I put my fingers on the problem switches and forcefully pulled them to the on position, never letting go. I was standing there dripping with sweat in the dark room, holding onto those switches for dear life. I couldn't even let them go for a second to turn on a light.

"I'll stand here as long as I have to in order to keep the power on, you bastard!" I hissed, nobody around to hear me. I stood there by myself pulling determinedly on those switches for an hour. Lunch was a success.

They certainly don't teach that in business school.

09

How to Burn an Inheritance

I DON'T LIKE TALKING ABOUT MONEY. Who does? It's something of a taboo subject in society, probably because people can use it as a weapon to "rank themselves" against others, which is a shitty thing to do. But money is also a reality problem; you need it to eat, live, and provide shelter. Anything beyond that is simply lifestyle choice. But I learned a lot of valuable lessons after receiving a small but significant inheritance from my father in the form of life insurance. Since no one likes to talk about it, here's the advice I would have given myself four years ago if I could go back and start over. Maybe others in my position will find it helpful.

The first challenge I faced was of guilt and confusion. This was my money, yet I hadn't done anything to deserve it. I didn't *earn* it. How was I supposed to feel? It put me in a moral quandary. But what I've learned with time is 1) nobody really cared except me, 2) lots of other people benefit from family generosity, and it's not a sin, and 3) what matters is whether you're motivated to accomplish things or not, irrespective of any "safety net" you may have. If your wealth is great enough, you can do this in the form of creating a private family foundation and overseeing how it gets disbursed to charities. The point is, there is no need to get insecure or defensive about it—just be appreciative, compassionate, and sensitive to others who may not

be in the same situation. If they judge you for it, that's simply a reason not to be their friend.

Money can cause lots of additional problems if you don't handle it wisely. It can cause family members to turn against one another, if they're not careful. Shortly after my father's death (while I was still grieving), I had to press charges against my own uncle because he was harassing my stepmother and me regarding Dad's estate. So, what should you do if you receive a large sum of money? The first thing you should do is absolutely nothing. I cannot stress this point strongly enough. You're most likely in a highly emotional and irrational state of mind. Whether you just won the lottery or just lost a family member, you have this newfound wealth you've never had before. DON'T DO ANYTHING. No emotional purchases: no fancy cars, no houses, no expensive jewelry. Don't do anything that will immediately change your existing lifestyle in any meaningful way. It's like liposuction; your problems will just quickly bounce back (okay, pun intended) in a different manifestation. Just take a deep breath, hire a psychologist, and take it easy for a few weeks or months. That's what I wish I'd done.

FINANCIAL ADVISOR

The second thing you should do is interview different financial advisors to find one you trust and start investing your money. This is very important. Ask friends for referrals (depending on the bank, most financial advisors require a minimum of $250K). Investing will allow you to do a couple of things:

1. You can create a line of credit (borrowed cash) at a very low interest rate against your assets. You can draw off this amount (usually 75 percent of your total assets) whenever you need to. Obviously, you'll have to pay it back eventually, or you could theoretically leave it and use dividend income to pay the interest, but I digress.

2. Dividend income. Depending on how your advisor chooses to build your portfolio (more aggressive and risky, longer time horizon and less need for cash now, vs. less risky, shorter time horizon, and more need for cash now), you'll earn money on top of your initial investment through your investments' dividends (payouts from stocks). These can vary widely depending on the index (collection of stocks) your advisor chooses, from 4 to 15 percent annually. Other macro/global/political factors can play a large role in determining this.

The advantage young people have is *time*. The more time you have, the more risky/long-term of a position you can take, since you'll live through many financial cycles (crashes and booms). Also, more time will allow you to compound your assets to a much greater amount over the course of several decades. All financial advisors love to use these "illustrations" as an advertising tool demonstrating how much money you could potentially have at sixty-five. Of course, the world never works in such a linear fashion. But we millennials have plenty of time to figure that out.

WILLS, TRUSTS, AND ESTATES

Hire a lawyer. It doesn't have to be the world's fanciest or most expensive, but there may be lots of future issues depending on the circumstances of your wealth. Over the last four and a half years, I've learned more about wills, trusts, and estate law than I ever wanted to. Here's the biggest lesson (both for receiving an inheritance and if you're planning one for yourself): non-probate versus probate. *Remember these words.* Non-probate means assets avoid the lengthy legal system and are distributed directly to the beneficiary (you). In non-probate, there's no room for discussion, disagreement, or interpretation.

Probate, on the other hand, means assets must be decided by a judge (even if everything is spelled out clearly in a will). Anything can happen in that scenario; random family members who are upset they weren't mentioned in the will can challenge it, or existing beneficiaries can make claims if they don't like the distribution. Certain types of assets are considered probate versus non-probate. For example, wills are always probate. Even if the will perfectly lays out in clear English how the deceased intends to disburse his or her money, it must still be approved by a judge in court.

Life insurance, on the other hand, is considered non-probate. It's a simple transaction; the name and amount are listed on the policy, and the recipient receives a check when you die, no questions asked. You want as much as possible to be set up as non-probate when planning your own estate—it makes everyone's lives a lot easier and less stressful and saves survivors a lot of money in potential legal fees after you're gone.

The other issue (and always a political hot topic) is concerning estate tax. Every state has different limits and rules regarding how much you can receive without paying taxes (in addition to federal limits). Anything beyond that is subject to federal estate tax. There's an important distinction that must be made on this point. Certain assets, such as life insurance, are not subject to income tax; however, when included in other things (assuming there's more to the estate than simply a life insurance policy, such as cars, houses, etc.), they're included in the aggregate total of the estate, which is taxable. For example, let's say I live in New York, and the estate limit is $10 million (that's not exactly accurate, but pretty close). I receive $5 million in life

insurance from a family member's death. I owe zero tax on that five million. Yippee! However, let's say that family member also owned an $8-million house that I'm also receiving. 8 + 5 = $13 million which is $3 million over the $10 million allowable threshold in New York. So, you owe taxes on the portion above the $10 million. Still a lot better than owing taxes on the full $13 million, but Uncle Sam was just invited to your party.

PURCHASING A HOUSE

One of the biggest decisions you'll make in your life is buying a home. It's a serious commitment, both emotionally and financially, and while it can be a very lucrative one over time, it can also be daunting for first-time home-buyers. Depending on the type of transaction, the whole process can be a lot more complex than it should be.

Real estate in New York City is a whole other animal. But in a post–Dodd-Frank banking environment and considering the real estate collapse of the early 2000s, there are certain things you need to know, which I learned the hard way. After my father passed away, I attempted to make an emotional housing purchase (yes, that's a big, impulsive purchase). I was in contract but had to pull out due to financing issues, and I paid a settlement. It was a mistake on my part for sure, but I also gained insight into a really fucked-up system. Here's what I discovered.

THE MORTGAGE PROCESS

Okay, so you found a house you love. Congratulations! Now you want to purchase it. Assuming you decide to finance the sale and not pay all in cash, then all you have to do is muster up 20 percent of the purchase price as a down deposit and get a mortgage for the rest! Right? Wrong. Let me explain.

For 95 percent of mortgage applicants, this may be correct. But the 5 percent who are recipients of newly inherited wealth are a unique category. No one explained this to me. In the post–housing crash of the early 2000s, Dodd-Frank was passed as a legislative measure that prevented banks from lending mortgages to "risky" applicants. Sounds smart, but in practice how this translates is that every bank has a checklist of criteria the applicant must meet in order to qualify for a mortgage. In fact, in a very egalitarian fashion, they don't even take into consideration the applicant as a person. They *only* consider your previous three years' tax returns.

For example, let's say you just graduated from Harvard Business School and for the sake of the argument, your parents own Nike (yes, the company). You have $3 million of your own money in the bank. You want to purchase a home that costs $2 million. Of course, you have the ability to pay cash for it, but you choose not to tie up so much of your resources into one purchase. You, Nike child, would *not* qualify for a mortgage. You are a "risky" applicant. Why? Your "annual income" is only $100,000. ($3 million / 30 years). They assume you will never work a day in your life and amortize the cash over thirty years.

Because this hypothetical applicant didn't have a job within the last two to three years, the bank has nothing to base their amount on. The applicant could have been the CEO of a company prior to starting business school, but that's irrelevant. Someone explain to me how this makes sense. From the bank's perspective, how is this person considered riskier than someone who has no savings, is earning a livable income, but could get fired at any moment and then be unable to make mortgage payments? This measure assumes this person is going to take his MBA, sit on it, and do nothing for the rest of his life. This is a broken system that desperately needs to be examined.

The biggest lesson I learned is that before you commit to buying a home, first go through the mortgage process and see how much you qualify for, *then* make your purchasing decision. Not the other way around. Also, "preapproval" for a mortgage doesn't mean shit. This is just a predatory tactic mortgage companies and brokers use to get your business. It holds no actual weight in the final underwriting process and decision-making.

THE CONTRACT

All you need to know about here is the non-financing contingency clause, which states that if you fail to qualify for a mortgage (see above) for any reason, *you're still legally obligated to pay for the apartment or house.* You need to be aware of this and be very careful if it's in your contract. You should fight to remove it, if possible, unless you're 1,000 percent certain you're going to buy the house.

LIFE INSURANCE

You're a millennial. You're invincible! You'll live to be at least 100 years old, right? So, why should you think about death at such an early age? Life insurance is the last thing on any young person's mind, and understandably so. But it shouldn't be.

Shortly after my parents were diagnosed with cancer, my former college roommate, who was working as an insurance agent at the time, came to me and said, "You know, Pete, god forbid anything happens to either of your parents in the future, you may not be eligible for a life insurance policy, or you might be considered 'risky' and have to pay insane premiums." Lo and behold, soon thereafter my father passed away. It was the best piece of advice I could have been given, and I'm eternally grateful for my friend's foresight.

The point is, regardless of whether your parents are sick, if you take out a life insurance policy early in life (even a very small one), it will compound and grow over time to a significant amount. Then you can live your life a little more stress-free, knowing that even in the worst-case scenario (you lose all of your money), you'll still have something remaining to give your family one day.

There are different kinds of life insurance policies. The one you want is whole life, not term. Term is what all those TV ads are selling; "For less than a dollar a day you can be covered for $250,000!" Yes, this is technically true, but you don't earn any money on this type of policy, and it doesn't grow over time. Whole life is a bit more expensive, but it will compound over many decades while you're living, plus give you a line of credit in case you need to borrow some cash against it. So, please, do yourself and your family a favor and take out a small whole life insurance policy. Your future children will thank you (and me).

The joys, trials, and pitfalls of dating in New York City and how to find and cultivate meaningful relationships

Soc

ial

Millennial

10

First Love Lost

I'**VE SPENT HUNDREDS OF HOURS AND THOUSANDS OF DOLLARS ON DATES OVER THE YEARS, BUT I HAVE ONLY EVER HAD ONE REAL GIRLFRIEND—A GIRL I'LL CALL ASHLEY—TO WHOM I WAS READY TO PROPOSE.** Interestingly, Ashley met my father before I met her, at a Lincoln Center charity gala two months prior to his death. Our relationship had deep emotional and psychological meaning—this was the last woman I would ever date who knew my father.

I couldn't breathe.

I was trying to suck in oxygen, but no amount seemed adequate (eerily similar to the way my father felt in the hours leading up to his death). I was standing in my kitchen with my phone in my right hand, trembling as I obsessively scrolled through photos of Ashley and me. She had decided to take a weeklong break before finally ending our relationship. It was so painful, it felt like someone had shoved an icepick right in the middle of my brain.

"Oh, baby, noooo! Oh god! Please don't go!"

I was having a panic attack. I could hear my father's voice in my head, "Peter, don't fuck this up! Don't lose this girl!" Ashley and I would never say the word "goodbye" to each other while dating. We didn't like the connotation, so opted instead to say "see you soon" after each date was over. But this time it was goodbye. I was crying uncontrollably and screaming, but no one was there to listen. I was all alone. I knew this feeling all too well; I was re-experiencing yet another major loss in my life. Except this time, it wasn't my father.

A few weeks back, I had been at an emotional crossroads; I had to

make a hard decision: do I continue operating the restaurant or close it and focus on my relationship? The long hours and mental stress of operating a restaurant in Manhattan had taken their toll on me and our relationship. So, ultimately, I chose Ashley, thereby shutting down the business for good. She broke up with me two weeks later, after dating for two and a half years. When my relationship with Ashley died, my father died all over again. She was a living "bridge" between us. I had failed Ashley, my father, and myself. And now I was unemployed and alone.

I had loved her, I just didn't realize how much until she was gone. There's a valuable lesson in this. Don't take anyone, or *anything*, for granted. Because they can be gone in an instant.

More importantly, my relationship with Ashley taught me what it means to truly be in love with another person. How to love someone and put another person's interests equal to (and at times above) your own. We were twenty-six when we started dating. So much life experience happens in your twenties. Women tend to mature more quickly than men, but I honestly thought I knew everything in my twenties, only to realize I knew jack shit when I turned thirty.

To be in love with someone means to appreciate who they are every single day, including all of their strengths and weaknesses. To love you for just being *you*. Is there such a thing as "love at first sight"? Eh, it's possible. But probably unlikely for the majority of us. It really takes time to get to know someone and build a deep connection. Does this person make you feel happy when you think of them? Do they make you smile at the thought of their image in your head? Do you miss them when they're gone? These are the intangible signs of love. Not fireworks and magical unicorns. *Love*.

Sometimes—oftentimes—we don't realize our mistakes until it's too late. Maybe they're incredibly subtle so you think it's not your fault: a sideways glance at a restaurant, a roll of the eyes, a personal silence in a crowded room where everyone else is talking. Maybe it's so subtle, it's not even physical. Maybe it's an indefinable feeling that crowds around you when you enter your home after a long and grueling day of work, finding your significant other already asleep in bed. Tomorrow morning there should be words exchanged: "Hey, I'm sorry I got home so late last night. I missed you. I think I'll put my manager on this week and take some time away. Would you like to join me?"

But if you say nothing and continue on that path of going to work and getting home late, of letting the silences deepen and the words remain hidden—eventually, the fissure between you will grow until you're too far apart. There are always warning signs, always things that signify you've taken a wrong turn and you're growing apart. You just need to be aware of them.

I've had three years to reflect on my past with Ashley, and two questions still remain: 1) Do I still love her? 2) If we met today, knowing what we know now and the lessons gained, would the outcome be any different?

Yes, I still have love for Ashley, but not in the same romantic way. I care about her in the same sense that I care for my friends and wouldn't want anything bad to happen to her. With or without me, I just want her to be happy. I appreciate her vibrant spirit and authenticity and feel a connection with her—I'm not sure that ever fully goes away.

Ashley played an important role in my life, for better or worse. There are very few people in this lifetime you'll really get to know on such an intimate level. You can probably count them on one hand. Make sure they know you appreciate them.

The more time that passes, however, the more I realize she is not *my person* in life. You have to stick with people through good times and bad, believing in their potential to change. I guess it's just a question of how long you're willing to wait to see change. In fairness, she stayed in it as long as she could, and I probably was very resistant to change. But I didn't know how to separate my father's voice from my own. And, unfortunately, sometimes change only happens after the trauma has occurred, and not before. Some people are meant to be in your life forever; some are meant to be there for a certain period of our lives to teach us something meaningful.

Whomever you're with next will appreciate this chapter of your life and trust you to be fully dedicated to them. If you can't fully trust each other, then nothing is going to be sustainable in the long-term. And if you're not fully dedicated, then you really shouldn't be dating someone until you're emotionally available. You need to be honest with your partner and, more importantly, with yourself. Falling out of love with someone can take years, not weeks or months. I see too many people trying to recreate past romance too soon simply because they miss the intimate connection they had with another human being. But this can't be rushed or forced. It's not the same as gluing back together a broken vase and pretending it's like new.

Love can be painful. In fact, it's some of the greatest pain we will experience in life. But we shouldn't put up walls to protect our fragile hearts and minds; doing so simply denies us of the natural beauty of being alive. Embrace love, share it with others, and don't ever be afraid to openly express your love in fear of it not being reciprocated. You need to remind yourself that you aren't doing it for others, but for yourself. *Your person* will naturally be drawn to your warmth and openness. And to the ones that aren't? Just express compassion, and politely ignore them.

11

An Epic Second Date

IONCE MET A GIRL, REBECCA, FOR COFFEE AFTER MATCHING ON A DATING APP (THE LEAGUE). It was a Monday at 5 p.m. Six hours later, we were booked on a flight to Buenos Aires, Argentina, leaving Friday. For our second date, I picked her up at her apartment building in a taxi, and we went to the airport. This is how it unfolded, and I'll share what I learned about the importance of taking spontaneous risks.

Rebecca's dating app profile boasted a unique personality, and when we matched on The League, I thought she'd be an interesting person with whom to have a conversation. We met on a Monday afternoon in Tribeca (lower Manhattan). What was supposed to be a quick introduction turned into a two-hour date. It felt like one of those rare moments when you form an immediate, deep connection with someone.

During the coffee date, one of the questions I asked was, "Hypothetically, if you could go to the airport *right now* and go anywhere in the world, where would you go and why?" (I like this question because it challenges the other person to narrow their thinking, and it captures what's important to them. Culture vs. beach, nature vs. metropolitan, developed countries vs. undeveloped, etc.) To be fully honest, I was so struck by her beauty that I wasn't paying much attention to her response. I think she said "Paris" because she loved the romantic nature of the city. She asked me the same question, and I responded "Tahiti," because I had recently seen photos of its gorgeous white sand beaches and tiny islands,

and I love exotic locations. We enjoyed a lovely conversation covering a wide range of topics, so absorbed in each other's energy, the rest of our surroundings faded into irrelevance. I never wanted it to end, but, finally, the date ended with a kiss goodnight before we went our separate ways.

[Six Hours Later]

I received a text from Rebecca at 11:41 p.m.

"Want to go to Tahiti Friday?"

"I could actually do that," I said. "Should I clear my schedule for next week? Be careful what you say, Rebecca."

"Be careful what *you* say, Peter."

I scratched my chin, thinking about it. Was she serious? Was I serious? "Ha. Challenge accepted. Give me the green light, and I'll book flights."

Rebecca sent a GIF of a flashing green light, followed by her passport number, date of birth, and known traveler number.

My sister and I received a lot of airline miles from American Airlines when our father passed away (thanks, Dad!), and I had been very careful in saving them. I was waiting for the right time to use a portion of them and thought this was as opportune a moment as ever. I called American Airlines immediately and spoke to a travel agent. Another interesting conversation ensued.

"Hi," I said, "I'd like to use miles to purchase two tickets from New York to Tahiti."

"When are you looking to travel?"

"Friday."

....

"Um, *this* Friday?" he asked.

"Yes."

"Unfortunately, we have a limited number of seats reserved for mileage tickets, and they were booked months ago. I don't have anything available for a while."

Figures, considering the number of honeymooners that book that flight. I scrambled to think of other destinations I wanted to go to but had never been. I remembered from my travel conversation with Rebecca that neither of us had ever been to South America before.

"How about New York to Buenos Aires, returning next Tuesday?"

I heard typing. "Yes, I have that available. It will be 55,000 miles per ticket for coach fare. However, I have a milesaver offer for two seats left in first class for 80,000 miles per ticket, if you're interested? These would usually go for 120,000 miles each."

"I'll take it."

I texted Rebecca and explained to her the location change (but not about first class; that was going to be a surprise). She was all for South America. I told her I'd pick her up at 7 p.m. at her apartment building and we could travel to the airport together.

I paused, taking a moment to think. I had just met this girl less than seven hours ago, and we were already booked to go to Buenos Aires on the most epic second date I had ever had. Talk about spontaneity.

The rest seems like a blur. I picked her up on Friday and immediately gave her a kiss. There was definitely some tension and nervousness in the air. Neither of us had ever done something like this before, and we certainly hadn't expected to be doing this five days ago when we first met. But that's what made it exciting. It was all new to us. It was risky. Unknown.

After we took off, everyone quickly fell asleep except for us. In first class, they had bucket seats that would swivel 180 degrees so we could face each other while having a luxury three-course meal with a dim "candlelight" lamp on our table. It was the most romantic setting in my entire life. I felt like I was in a movie.

We had a lovely weekend together. We learned how to play polo. We learned how to dance tango. We toured the entire city. Everything—from the beauty and squalor of the city to the fresh scents of Argentine food—was new, exciting, different. Just like each moment spent with this beautiful stranger. It was a time of intense discovery compressed into less than a week. When you spend that much time with someone in a different country, you learn a lot about that person. We laughed, we cried. By the end of it, I felt like I had known Rebecca for years.

Arriving back in New York, I dropped her off at her apartment and we exchanged some kind words to each other. There wasn't a third date. I've spent a lot of time analyzing this experience and reliving it in my head and have come up with several key takeaways. Life is all about timing. In that moment, I honestly don't think she was ready for a serious relationship. She had just gotten out of a long-term relationship and just wanted to go on an adventure with someone.

However, to be fair, there was a double-sided risk. While it might be easy to criticize and suggest that she shouldn't be taking trips with guys if she's not emotionally available without communicating that prior, I also shouldn't be enabling this kind of behavior without first learning about someone's intentions or communicating expectations. No one is to blame. There is absolutely nothing wrong with going on spontaneous trips. Life is an adventure, and you can't live it with regret. I think we both were looking for a sense of adventure; we were just in different emotional stages at the time. In the moment, however, it felt right. And if nothing else, it was an experience we will share for the rest of our lives.

Take risks. Be bold. And don't care what others think or worry about being judged. People are going to judge you no matter what, so just embrace life and live it the way you want, because you only get one life. First free yourself of these psychological barriers, then you can free others. You create your own reality.

12

How to Be a Dream Man

IN THE SPRING OF 2009, BEFORE GRADUATION, THE ENTIRE SORORITY CHAPTER OF DELTA DELTA DELTA VOTED ME UNANIMOUSLY AS THEIR "TRI-DELTA DREAM MAN," A SYMBOLIC GESTURE BESTOWED UPON ONE MALE UNDERGRADUATE REPRESENTATIVE OF THEIR SORORITY. I was extremely honored and humbled to be given this award. As silly as it might seem at face value, it was reflective of a deeper trust and connection that 100+ women shared with me. Reflecting back, it was a life-altering moment, because it gave me the self-confidence that I could be a leader; not in the typical business setting we're accustomed to, but a leader among men, a leader in principles and values. That's the true sign of a leader. I want to share my insights with my male counterparts on how they too can be a leader. Hopefully I'll inspire and encourage them to act in a better way toward other people and, most importantly, toward themselves.

As silly as it may sound, I take a lot of pride in having been voted a sorority "Dream Man" while attending the University of Miami in South Florida. I was extremely humbled by this honor and took my title very seriously—it wasn't some kind of conquest or achievement, but an appreciation of the way I

treated women.

It all started after I briefly dated a girl (let's call her Jennifer) who was a member of the Delta Delta Delta (aka Tri-Delta) sorority. I treated her like a princess, but, despite multiple warnings from other people, I remained naïve to the fact that she was essentially using me for nice things like fancy dinners and concerts, while also hitting on other guys and talking to her ex-boyfriend behind my back.

By that time, I had become good friends with many of her sorority sisters. When Jennifer's behavior finally came to the surface, rather than sticking with her, as I assumed sorority sisters naturally would do, they realized how poorly she had treated me and chose to remain friends with me instead. This wasn't an intentional play on my part, but there is some irony in it. I guess the saying is true, "What goes around comes around."

Over the course of the next two years, I got to know almost every girl in the sorority, and they constantly invited me to their events. I always spoke highly of their organization to others on campus, and those girls became some of my best friends. When I was about to graduate, they honored me at formal by unanimously nominating me as their "Dream Man" for 2009 (similar to a fraternity "sweetheart.") They made me a beautiful custom shirt with their Greek letters stitched on the front, and DREAM MAN printed on the back. It was purely symbolic, but I was humbled and appreciative.

This was no easy feat. Remember, this is Greek life in college—constant drama. At times, I felt like I was dating more than 100 girls at once. Someone would talk to me about another girl in the same sorority, and I just had to listen. When emotions get involved, you have to be extremely careful not to offend anyone or do anything considered inappropriate. Otherwise the news will spread like wildfire, and you'll just as quickly be exiled forever. Trust me, it's a high-stakes game of emotional poker. So how do you win over the hearts of 100 women in the same organization or social circle?

Very. Fucking. Carefully.

Before I share what I learned about how to treat women so that they love and adore you, let me share a few things you *shouldn't* do. You know how you don't become a Dream Man to 100 women? By acting like a bro.

DO NOT CALL ME "BRO." I AM NOT YOUR BRO.

"Hey bro! What's your problem?"

When did it become socially acceptable to address people in such a fashion? I've come to believe that 95 percent of interpersonal communication problems derive from a general lack of maturity in our society. A person's maturity level isn't necessarily dictated by their age—I've met twenty-three-year-olds who act like they're thirty, and forty-five-year-olds who act like they're twelve. The real issue is how we choose to conduct ourselves and what standards we hold ourselves to.

The greatest contributors to a high maturity level are upsetting life experiences and the mental framework we use for coping with pain and tackling difficulties when they arise. Do you sweep issues under the rug or do you face them head on? Can you own your thoughts and feelings, or do you lash out at those around you?

Why do so many men behave in immature ways, anyhow? To me, it's simple: they lack any semblance of emotional maturity. Immature guys think a display of power and ego is what girls want, when in fact these displays are nothing more than overcompensation born from insecurity. Men are so focused on impressing other men that they lose sight of the real goal, which is to have a loving relationship with yourself and with someone else. And yes, maybe some girls do want that kind of blowhard, but not the good ones, the self-respecting ones, those with a strong and healthy sense of self. Healthy women see straight through a man who's just trying to impress other people.

Another gauge of maturity is how well someone treats other people once he or she has a measure of money and success. As an example, you know who are total bros? New York City finance guys. Ladies, let me clue you in: if your date works in finance, there's a 99 percent chance he is not a dream man, but a total douchebag. Sorry.

Now, I have friends in finance, and both my parents worked in financial services, so I'm not out to stereotype the entire bunch. But I've seen what the culture does to people, and this group of men is overwhelmingly ... bad. I don't like the way they talk about women. They're chauvinists. "Hey, bro, like, how many chicks did you bang this weekend?" It's so fucking immature, so childish. At the end of the day, it's counterproductive to what you're actually trying to do, which is to win over women, not your fellow "bros."

A lot of women I've met in New York City are particularly jaded from dating men in finance and the power and money struggles that accompany them. New York is an expensive city to live in—women who might not make a ton of money enjoy dinner at upscale restaurants or a luxurious vacation provided by one of these guys. They may want to assume the best of these men, but they don't realize that they have a hidden agenda—they use their money as a means to get what they want. It's easy for both men and women to get enamored by that lifestyle, especially when some women will throw themselves at you if you flash the cash.

I watch women fall at the feet of guys who have lots of money to spend. They get wined and dined and treated like shit. This abuse just kicks up whatever unresolved wounds someone has from childhood and past relationships. I've had dates with these jaded souls—one such young woman arrived at my apartment drunk and insecure and accusing me of abandoning her before our first date was over. If I were to estimate, I'd say about 85 percent of the women I've gone out with in the past few years are like this—too wounded to have healthy relationships at all.

I can hear it now: "No, man, don't blame us for the nutty women you meet. Women are crazy." I hear this statement a lot, from both men and women, actually. I've spent a lot of time analyzing this, so let's solve the myth once and for all. Is it true that women are "crazy"? The answer is, yes, sometimes, but it's not women's fault. It originated with men.

Generally speaking, most of these women started out sane and normal. They were doing just fine over the course of their young lives, unless they had an asshole for a dad, in which case the trouble started even earlier. But then they came across a few really bad guys who treated them poorly. After having several such negative dating experiences, they downloaded and internalized the idea that this behavior was true of most, if not all, men.

And because they haven't mentally compartmentalized the few bad actors, these women subconsciously let the assholes ruin it for all other future good men they might come across.

So, yeah, a lot of women *are* "crazy," but it's generally the fault of guys, starting way back when her father was emotionally unavailable right down to her most recent date with some egotistical asshole in finance who treated her like shit. This is unfortunate for the woman because she often fails to recognize a good guy when she comes across one, instead categorizing him by default as no better than the others who came before him. In this default safety mode, she misses out on some great opportunities. On behalf of all good men, I sincerely apologize for these assholes. Trust me, I'd like to get rid of them also.

BEING A DREAM MAN

This kind of immaturity is why I have more female than male friends. I love being surrounded by women. Maybe I'm a little too woman-crazy, a little too in love with them. But this is not a game to me. I'm not manipulative. I've earned their trust. And that's because I lead with my heart; I don't have any hidden agenda or ulterior motives.

Being a Dream Man isn't about manipulating the hearts and minds of women into thinking you're a good guy. It has to stem from trust, respect, and emotional maturity. What does it mean to be mature? I would like to propose a radical new concept (well, radical to some). Maturity means being able to take a wider approach to problems and to be less emotionally reactive. To *listen*. To express yourself and show vulnerability. To be in touch with your feelings. Most importantly, maturity is about being an independent thinker. Maturity is not buying into group mentality; it's calling someone out when they do something inappropriate. Be humble. Be appreciative. Show compassion.

Treat women and all people with respect.

What is immaturity, then? Making fun of people. Projecting your insecurities onto others. Making yourself feel better by dragging other people down. Making sexual or inappropriate jokes. There's no place for that in society. How exactly do you accomplish maturity? By actively choosing to hold yourself accountable to a higher standard, even when no one's watching. It requires extreme discipline but will create less drama and stress in your life.

Now let's talk about how to truly win over women. Gentlemen, I hope you're reading this part very carefully. There are many temptations you'll have to fight off. Here are some ground rules.

1. If you treat girls nicely, they will reciprocate and treat you nicely back (I know, what a revolutionary concept!). So, don't be a jerk. And if a girl *doesn't* treat you nicely, you should still treat her nicely. Be the bigger person. Don't stoop to her level. Just keep a smile on your face.

2. Girls talk. Expect that everything you say and do will get around and spread. Just pretend you have a microphone and camera on you at all times. I don't care how close of friends you think you are with someone— girls form a protective bond greater than can be achieved with any male. So be mature and on your best behavior at all times. If you're thinking of doing something stupid or saying something crass, err on the side of caution. You can do that silly stuff with your guy friends later.

3. This is the hardest one for a guy, but if you can accomplish this, you're golden. Don't sleep around with girls in the same social circle. Believe it or not, after my experience with Jennifer, I didn't date a single girl in that sorority. I'm not suggesting you can't date anyone, but if you choose to hook up with someone, you'd better be damn sure going into it that you genuinely like the person. Choose very wisely. Don't just hook up with someone for fun within the same group. There are three billion other women in the world—can't you have fun with someone else? Let me tell you, there's no faster way of being ousted from an organization or social circle and putting all that social capital to waste than randomly hooking up with a girl and never talking to her again. And if you're going to break up, do it in the most responsible, respectful, and gentlemanly fashion known to humankind. Treat it like brain surgery. I cannot emphasize this enough.

It boils down to this: treat girls with respect. Don't be the source of any drama. And be their public advocate. Do that, my friend, and you'll be rewarded handsomely. Conversely, mess up, and good luck finding your next girlfriend. New York City is a smaller town than you think.

13

Reality Dating

IN THE FALL OF 2011, FILMING BEGAN FOR A NEW REALITY TELEVISION SHOW CALLED *GALLERY GIRLS* TO BE FEATURED ON BRAVO NETWORK. It chronicled the lives of seven ambitious young women in New York City trying to make it in the uber-competitive art gallery world. Amy, one of my closest friends from college, was one of the featured cast members on the show. She had invited me to numerous events to be filmed, but I respectfully declined each time. Then one day she sent me a text: "Would you be willing to stage an on-screen romance with me?" I responded, "What exactly does that entail?" And so the story goes...

Let me preface by saying that I love Amy to death. She remains a dear friend today. I was twenty-five at the time, and my parents weren't big fans of reality TV. Amy had hosted several dinners and parties for friends to be taped, and she'd invited me several times. I was very hesitant, too concerned with my reputation and fear of being judged. I also knew full well that these shows have the creative license to edit footage however they please. But because Amy was a good friend of mine, I also felt bad constantly declining; I wanted to help her with this new endeavor. So, when she texted, "Would you be willing to stage an on-screen romance with me?" I agreed to go on a date with her. Based on my limited knowledge of reality TV shows, none of which I was comfortable with, I was envisioning black-and-white night-vision cameras in her bedroom.

I arrived at the restaurant at exactly 7 p.m. The producers installed a microphone inside my shirt, and I sat down at the table with a bright filming light thrust to the front-right side of my face. Amy was my friend, but we were pretending this was a first date.

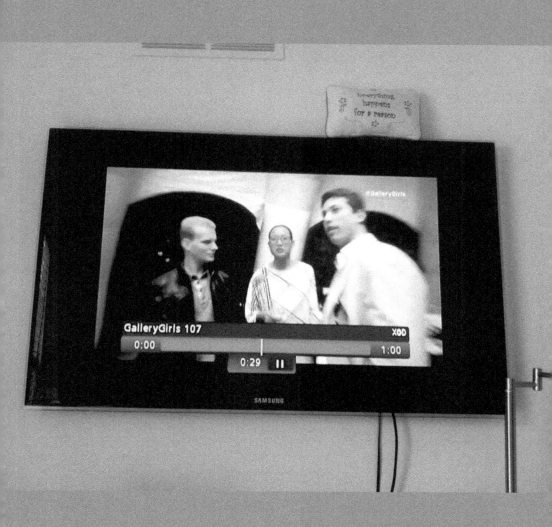

The dialogue was excruciating. "Where are you from? Where did you grow up? That's so nice. Hahahaha." It felt very awkward; you could cut the tension with a knife. As we proceeded through our phony questioning (nothing was scripted, in case you were wondering), Amy stood up and headed to the bathroom. A few short moments later, the lead producer unexpectedly sat down in Amy's chair in front of me.

"Peter, you need to man up. You need to kiss Amy!"

I laughed, baffled. "We shall see. I'm not sure how it'll play out."

But the producer was persistent. I could see in his eyes that it would be a huge disappointment if I didn't kiss Amy. The pressure was on.

I'm not stupid. I had known this moment was going to come and had already given it some thought. Frankly, that wasn't the kind of fame I was looking for. Plus, I didn't have a crystal ball—who knew who might come into my life six months in the future? I was trying to avoid having a difficult conversation with my hypothetical girlfriend when this show aired months later.

"Uh, Peter? Why are you on TV kissing a random girl?"

"That's, uh . . . she's . . . well . . . I can explain. Nothing else happened, I swear."

SLAP!

So, I already knew I was going to decline a kiss with Amy. My future relationship depended on it. But in hindsight, I should have done it just for the fun of it. Amy sat back down at the table and immediately lunged forward to give me a quick kiss. I think our lips connected for about 0.25 seconds before I awkwardly pulled back. This girl wasn't messing around; she meant business. After another brief pause and awkward silence, I tried to pretend that didn't happen and proceed with finishing dinner. What do you say in that situation? Let me check the manual. After dinner, Amy and I stood on the street outside the restaurant; the camera guys were standing inside the front door, shooting through the windows to capture the dark silhouettes of our bodies.

"Well, I had a really fun time!" Amy said brightly.

"Me too! We should do it again sometime."

She slowly bent in for another kiss. I began to lean in too—*maybe I should just do it*. I just couldn't take the awkwardness anymore. I was about to kiss her, and at the last moment, I turned my head and gave her a kiss on the cheek. "Goodnight, Amy," I whispered, and walked away. The cameramen were stunned.

That scene ended up on the cutting room floor. It wasn't intentional on my part. I really just wasn't feeling the moment. I think if I'd kissed her, it would have made it on TV (although I would argue this makes for better television?). There were other brief cameos that did make the air, including during the season finale at Art Basel in Miami. Suffice to say, my TV days were over . . . or so I thought.

Immediately after my difficult breakup with Ashley, I felt a bit passionless for a period of time. It was hard to find motivation to do normal activities, and I just needed to take a real break from society and dating. Unfortunately, this went on for a while, and I was trying to think of things that would re-excite me. Unsure of myself, and after much internal deliberation, I decided to apply to *The Bachelorette* and created a short video to submit to the producers. I didn't think much of it, and as the months went on I forgot about it completely.

[Three months later]

My cellphone rings:

"Hi, is this Peter? This is Mark calling from ABC, on behalf of *The Bachelorette* casting."

(My voice a little shaky) "Hi, Mark. Yes, uh, this is Peter. How may I help you?"

"We apologize in the delay getting back to you. We would love to meet you and learn more about you for the upcoming season. Are you still single?"

Moment of truth. Do I lie and pass up this opportunity? Or go for it? "Thanks for the call, Mark! Yes, I am still single. I am based in New York City, though. Are you in California?"

"Yes, we are. However, we will be in Manhattan in two weeks and can set it up for then!"

"OK, great."

Two weeks later, I sat down with the team inside a hotel room at the Roosevelt Hotel in Midtown Manhattan. They instructed me to dress "as if I was going on a first date." Inside the room, there were several cameramen, the casting director, and her assistant. We had a thirty-minute conversation, with lots of cameras and a bright photography light shining on my face (after my previous experience with Amy, this felt all too familiar). She asked me a wide range of questions. "Explain to me an ideal first date." "Why do you believe you're still single?" "What qualities do you look for in a woman?" The list went on and on. I tried to answer as succinctly and respectfully as I could. The interview ended with, "Thank you so much. We'll let you know if we're interested." And that was it.

I never did receive a callback. I'm not upset about it. I share these stories to illustrate how easy it is for our generation to get caught up obsessing over image and perfection (myself included!). Many millennials have stupidly unrealistic expectations for the people they date based on what we see on television, and those impossible standards are robbing us all of a chance at real love. We're so worried about being judged—or what our friends think of who we're dating—that we lose our own identities in the process.

Do these silly shows have entertainment value? Yes, absolutely. There is nothing wrong with that! Just be careful not to take them too seriously; otherwise, people might not take you too seriously, either.

14

It's Not You, It's New York City

FOR ME, THIS IS IT. THE BIG ONE. THE REASON, IF FOR NOTHING ELSE, THAT YOU SHOULD BUY THIS BOOK. I have insight into a wide variety of topics; some of them are more intuitive, while others are heavily steeped in experience. After my hard breakup in 2015, I "serial dated" for a period of time. As previously mentioned, I've spent hundreds of hours (and many thousands of dollars) on dates. While it's not necessarily a statistic I'm proud of, the fact is I have extensive insight into this subject. I've interviewed and discussed with friends, hosted talks, and generally been open-minded. I've gained an incredible wealth of knowledge about dating (as any of my friends can corroborate). I'll try my best to succinctly summarize my scientific data for you. The best part? This information will cost you less than a fancy drink at a bar.

This chapter, due to its sensitive nature, requires a preface: this is my experience and observation, based on millennial behavior and growing up and living in New York City. Your experiences may be very different from mine. I'll try my best not to offend or "categorize" anyone, but, to be honest, it's impossible to discuss this topic without doing so to some degree. I truly apologize in advance if I offend anyone, but I certainly welcome disagreement. The point of writing

Peter D.

32 • NoHo • 6' 2"

About Me   Sweet, caring, motivated, empathic, smart, funny, mature. Passionate about health and wellness! Love meeting new people and exploring life

Education   University of Miami • Babson College - Franklin W. Olin Graduate School of Business • St. Paul's School

Profession   Former Founder/Owner @ Darrow's Farm Fresh • Investor @ Startup Rounds • Investor @ HigherMe

this book is not to stir up controversy, but to provide a spark for passionate conversation and healthy discussion. I like to believe I'm actually "one of the good ones." Not a bad actor contributing to the problem, but you can be the judge of that. I'm just calling a spade a spade, as I see it. I believe, however, that despite being confined to New York City, most of the lessons can be applied universally across the dating spectrum, no matter what city or country you live in.

Dating in New York City is a different animal, a unique beast unlike any experience in the world. There's a multitude of reasons. First, there are so many people, for one. Second, New Yorkers tend to be a very motivated bunch; they attend many different events, conferences, and discussions, so literally everywhere you go, you meet new people. You're likely to meet hundreds of new people, thousands even, in the course of a year. And, for some reason, I find that an overwhelming majority of these people are single. Can it really be that difficult to find a partner?

Another unique element to dating in New York City is that things seem to start much later in life here compared to the rest of the U.S. In most places, it's socially expected that you're going to meet someone in the town you grew up in, settle down, and start a family. Many people get married and have kids at quite an early age. New York is the opposite. It's a transient city. Most people aren't originally from New York. As a matter of fact, it's a very expensive place to live. People are busy building careers, and schools can be extremely expensive, as I've mentioned.

For these reasons, most people don't settle down until they're deeper into their career and more financially stable. For most men, this can be mid to late thirties, or even early forties. What's happening in between moving to New York and establishing your career? A term most people outside of Manhattan don't understand: casual dating. What is casual dating? It's when you're working really hard, you're extremely busy, you're constantly meeting new people, and settling down just isn't a priority at the moment. Is this fair to other people? No. This is simply what I observe. It's also generational; our parents don't understand this concept. I love the classic parental question, "Are you seeing anyone?" Yeah, Mom, ten people. Ask me again next month, it will probably be a different ten. Would I like there to be only one? Sure, of course I would. That's just not what I'm experiencing.

The problem is that women (especially the cute ones) are getting bombarded by men all the time. Everywhere they go, men are talking to them, hitting on them, sliding into their DMs. So, it's easily understandable that women don't know how to separate the bad from the good. This will eventually reveal itself with time, but the problem is women in New York City are often too quick in their decision-making. Obviously, you need to be attracted to the person in question, and efficient with your time. But my experience has been that women are too fast in "pulling the trigger" and don't give men ample time to show who they really are. They cut things off too soon. The window of opportunity is too small.

In New York, women tend to be overly concerned with what their friends think. A guy must require their friends' approval. Why, I ask? Who are you doing this for, you, or your (probably single) friends? Who made them the queens of dating? What's their track record? Are they really the best to be giving advice? If you like someone, and they make you happy, then who cares what your friends think? It's not like they're going to be dating that person.

"He's not good enough for you," is not a sufficient answer. Get rid of this concept of hierarchy; no one is "better" than anyone else. Every relationship dynamic is unique. I often hear, "I'm out of their league." I dislike this comment because it's one of the most widely practiced misconceptions in the dating world. Who the hell *are you*, the President of the United States? Don't be so self-righteous. Either they MAKE YOU HAPPY OR THEY DON'T. It's just a question of what core values are important to you. Does it matter if they know the capital of Arkansas? Or have a certain political stance? Don't be so detailed. How about just whether or not they're intellectually curious and motivated to learn? Do *you*. Don't worry about other relationships or people, just focus on yourself.

The other problem with New York City dating is the notion that there may be someone better out there for you than the person you're currently with. Get this out of your head. Otherwise you'll get caught in an abyss of selfishness where nothing and nobody is ever good enough, and you'll never be happy. Go with your gut feeling. Is there only one person in the world for you? No. Maybe there are 100. Any of the 100 will be fine. As you contemplate leaving someone for something better, chances are good that you're simply splitting hairs. The world of dating apps has contributed to this problem. They make it seem like finding a new person is as easy as swiping right. Finding a romantic interest is supposed to be difficult. If switching partners were easy, then the inherent value of relationships would become meaningless.

I find that many (but certainly not all) women fit into one of two categories: 1) Women who are dating aimlessly just for the sake of dating and have no idea what they're really looking for. Maybe they just got out of a long-term relationship and are restarting the dating scene after a long hiatus. We've all been there. You have to meet a lot of people and "kiss a lot of frogs" to figure out what you want. It just sucks to be on the receiving end of that. Or, 2) women looking for something perfect, who have a long checklist. You can often tell who these women are right away, because they may ask a lot of personal questions in rapid fire, such as, "Where did you go to college?" or, "What's your religion?" They have forty boxes to check, and if you hit only thirty-nine out of forty, sorry, you fail.

It's crucial that you be emotionally available and in the right headspace if you want to date with any semblance of success. I find that, on average, anyone younger than twenty-seven is too young to be ready for serious dating. A lot of crucial life experience occurs between twenty-two and twenty-seven years old.

When it comes to relationships, personally, I don't judge you by where you come from or what family you were born into. I'm not judgmental when it comes to the path you took to get here (although I'm certainly interested in it). All I care about is that you're here now. But it's important for you to be able to match me intellectually and emotionally. What I care about most are your intentions. Are you a good person? Are you trying to push yourself to learn from past mistakes? We're all flawed human beings. All we can do is make mistakes, learn from them, and hope not to repeat them (or not repeat them so severely). I care about one thing: us. Our connection. Nothing else matters.

So, exactly where and how do you meet *good* people? And what do you say? Let's be clear: there exist both amazing men and amazing women. Contrarily, there are also plenty of shitty men and shitty women. The challenge is not only to get two amazing people together, but also to have them feel a romantic spark. Often you can have two amazing people who on paper look great together, but they just don't seem to vibe or fit well. That's okay. I tend to find higher-quality people around intellectual activities where the focal point is something meaningful, rather than alcohol-based. This could include art museums, meditation groups, entrepreneurial events, community service fundraisers, etc. This doesn't mean you can't find your future spouse at a bar; I just think it's statistically more difficult.

HOW A GIRL BECOMES ENAMORED WITH YOU

If you're attracted to a girl, be bold and unafraid of rejection. Chances are she's single, and if she's not, she'll be flattered regardless. I know this is difficult for men and their ego; no one likes to hear "no". But you miss 100 percent of the shots you don't take in life.

Exactly what you say depends on the situation. Regardless, you have a very tight window of opportunity, maybe twenty seconds at best. Most of the time, I just go over and introduce myself. "Hi. I'm Peter." Then I extend my arm for a handshake. If it's a non-social situation, such as a coffee shop, on the street, sitting on a train, etc., this requires a little more finesse. I might open with something like, "Sorry to bother you, but do you have any recommendations on what to order? I've never been here before." Look her directly in the eye. Body language determines everything. If she's interested, she'll likely be conversational. "I love the scones, they're my favorite. Where are you from?" After a few seconds of chitchat, I'd say, "It would be fun to get a coffee or drink sometime, if you're free?" The "free" question is an important one; it's a code word for "single."

Just use normal conversation, and always be respectful. Here's what *not* to do: don't use cheesy pickup lines. Don't be weird or creepy. Don't say anything sexually suggestive or make any comment that could be misinterpreted as such in the slightest. We know you think she's hot, but learn to control yourself, dude! And please, *never* be disrespectful if you get a negative response.

HOW TO GO ON A DATE

If you're on a first date with a girl, you have only two tasks (other than being charming): 1) Make her feel comfortable. People feed off energy; if you're awkward, then it will feel awkward. Don't make any judgmental comments, even if she says something you may disagree with. Respond along the lines of, "That's an interesting way to look at it." She should be able to express herself freely without criticism. 2) Make her feel special (she is special!). Make her feel like she's the most important person in the world at that moment. Don't use your phone or text anyone. Her time is precious, so respect it.

Which brings me to my next point: be respectful. Always. Who taught you it's okay to treat women poorly? Your parents? Doubtful. Where did you get the notion that this is acceptable behavior? Your Neanderthal friends? Forget them. Be kind and complimentary. I know it's hard to express your feelings, but a simple, "I love that necklace," or, "You have beautiful eyes," can go a long way when it comes to first impressions. Women often expend a lot of effort to look good for a date; they'll appreciate it when you acknowledge this. Open the car door for her, offer your jacket if she's cold, always offer your arm and help her down the stairs. Don't walk in front of her, but beside her. Did chivalry die with millennials?

Early relationships can be confusing, especially after the first few dates. You might feel like you're ready to tie the knot after a month—that's new love for you. But it's important to learn how to control these emotions. Have a wider scope; this isn't the one-day stock market snapshot. It's the twelve-month snapshot. It's great to be excited about someone! All I'm suggesting is that it doesn't need to be up and down like a roller coaster. Be steady. Calm. It takes time to really get to know someone. Yes, you can often tell within the first ten minutes of meeting someone whether you want to get to know them more. But it takes more like three to six months to *really* get to know them. How do they treat you in social situations—are they inclusive? Do they make an effort to introduce you?

Just try to remember that there's no need to rush into things. Relationships are like building houses; a house built with wet concrete and a weak foundation will easily crumble. As fast as you built it, it can fall down. But a house built slowly with a strong foundation will last a lifetime. You want slow, sustained emotions built over time.

Here's the bottom line on dating: the point of relationships is to learn from each other, not to be codependent or needy. "I need X from my partner in order to be happy." As if there's some secret contract they're signing (that no one will ever be capable of fulfilling). Focus on giving yourself 100 percent of what *you* need, not 80 percent while expecting the other 20 percent to come from your partner.

Don't play games. Be authentically you. Don't change your swing in the middle of the pitch or try to be someone you think your partner wants. If they're the right person, they'll appreciate you for who you are. Toxic relationships suck energy; it's a race to the bottom. Don't make yourself feel better by bringing other people down—rather, build each other up. Push each other to be the best person you can be. And support each other when you're down. Be able to adapt. The person you are today is not the person you were five years ago, nor the person you will be five years from now.

I'll leave you with an interesting story. I'm not a professional dater. However, in October of 2017, I purchased a limited-offer, one year "unlimited" pass to The League, a popular dating app focused on an educated set. Essentially, for $1,000 I had unlimited access to as many swipes, power moves, and direct messages as I wanted; I had access to their entire database of beautiful, educated, single women in New York City. Understandably, I was using this newly discovered super-human ability to its full potential. I had something that very few other people had. I was burning through "tickets" (the currency that users would normally purchase at $3.50/ticket in order to use features of the app) at an incredible rate. Instead of only seeing three "potential matches" every day, like most users, I could see hundreds.

Word of this quickly spread to the executive headquarters. Not only did they immediately remove that unlimited product from the Apple Store for others to purchase, but they attempted to renege and yank my unlimited pass. I remembered reading about a similar story. In the 1980's, a struggling American Airlines offered the "AAirpass" in an attempt to quickly raise revenue. For approximately $250,000 (keep in mind this was the mid '80s), you had an unlimited, all-you-can-fly first-class ticket for the rest of your life (I believe Mark Cuban has one). It was an incredible mistake after they realized how much customers were exploiting it by flying millions of miles in a year, costing the airlines a ton of money. They too tried to yank the passes, only to be sued and lose. Inspired by that story, I politely responded to The League that I was going to sue them as a class action lawsuit for breach of contract. After some "negotiation," they backed down.

I met a lot of interesting people and had my share of fun. I also spent a lot more money on dating than I realized when looking at my bank account. In September of 2018, when the contract expired, I asked for a summary and overall "ranking" of my activity on The League compared to all of its users globally. Their response:

League Concierge: Hey Peter! Happy to help. Since this time last year, you've used 6,766 Tickets. To break it down even further you've used 1,599 tickets on Power Moves, 1,502 tickets on Power Move messages, 369 tickets for Rematches, 3,204 tickets for Extra Batches, 47 tickets on Undos, and 45 tickets on Profile Boosts. As for similar arrangements, you were in the top three of ticket users. I hope this helps!

If you do quick math, at $3.50/ticket I received a $23,681 value for only $1,000 spent. That's the best ROI (return on investment) that I've ever had in my life.

As I mentioned before, I'm not necessarily proud of this statistic. However, I have nothing to be ashamed of. In fact, the statistic I am most proud of is "0"; this is the total number of women who flagged or blocked me on the app, despite my heavy usage. I was always incredibly respectful and polite to all of my potential matches and real-life dates. I was never salacious and never did anything inappropriate. I didn't do anything illegal or immoral; all I am guilty of is looking for love.

But what I learned by the end of the twelve-month contract is that despite meeting a lot of people, I still felt lonely. I think psychologically this behavior, if anything, revealed the extent of the injury with which my ex-girlfriend Ashley left me. I thought I could heal myself by filling this void and going on a ton of dates. Ultimately, I learned that this was not a healthy approach. When it was time to renew, I respectfully declined. It's really about focusing your energy on quality people, not quantity. I am proud to say that those days are behind me. But it took a lot of personal reflection and struggle to realize that I was searching for a quick fix to a much deeper injury.

FOUR KEY LESSONS IN LOVE

1. Don't be afraid to be vulnerable. It's the only way you'll ever find what you need.

2. Treat people the way you want to be treated. Duh.

3. Focus on core values. Remember what's really important, and what's really not.

4. Remember that you attract the energy you put out into the universe. What you project will come back to you, so be intentional with your thoughts, words, and actions.

Evolution is often misunderstood as the "survival of the fittest," when in fact it's "survival of the most adaptable"

Resil

ient

Millennial

15

The Modern Family

IT WAS THE SUMMER OF 2005 WHEN MY PARENTS DECIDED THEY WERE GOING TO GET A DIVORCE AFTER BEING MARRIED FOR TWENTY-FIVE YEARS (OF COURSE, IT DIDN'T ACTUALLY BECOME OFFICIAL UNTIL A LITTLE LATER, DUE TO AN ARCHAIC LAW IN THE STATE OF NEW YORK THAT REQUIRES A ONE-YEAR MINIMUM OF SEPARATION BEFORE YOU CAN FINALIZE ANYTHING). At the time, both my sister and I were over the age of eighteen, so thankfully no custody agreement was required. Initially, the divorce was difficult for me to process. However, I've since had plenty of time to reflect on this period in my life and now have some succinct observations that I believe are worth sharing.

Given the sensitivity of this topic and the fact that real family members are involved, I'm going to try to speak in more general terms, rather than go into the specifics of my family's case. (Who really cares about the nitty-gritty details anyway? Every situation is different.)

I must admit, I was surprised to hear my parents wanted to get a divorce. Like every couple, they would have their fights once in a while, but by no means did I think it had reached an intolerable level. My thinking on this subject has shifted dramatically over the years. Initially I was more focused on the effects divorce has on the children. Now I'm more interested in the concept of divorce. Why do people *get* divorced? What changes

114

in a relationship? Why do people fall out of love? What's the threshold for change? Why did a certain couple get married in the first place? What was it about someone that you once loved, but no longer do? And to take it one step further, given that divorce rates are so high in this country and still trending upward, why are we so bad at choosing the "right" person?

As to the former, I can address the effects on children. Initially, it can be confusing to a child. There are several emotional stages, including anger, sadness, apathy, and plenty of blame. For the first six months I refused to say "I love you" back to my mother any time we would end a phone call or otherwise. I was upset and acting very immature, which I regret. Eventually, I realized all I wanted was for both my parents to be happy. While I'm entitled to my opinion, the fact is that my opinion really doesn't matter. It's not my life; it's theirs. Just because I don't like something doesn't mean I can expect them to make decisions solely to appease me. And even if they aren't happy, that's still not my problem. I have to focus on my life, not someone else's, regardless of whether they're family. Easy to say, very hard to do.

On the upside, there are some perks in the life of a child with divorced parents. You get double everything—double vacation opportunities, double presents around the holidays, etc. And each parent is discretely vying for your attention! I'm somewhat joking here, but I do find it fascinating how the vacation ideas all of a sudden get a lot more exotic and interesting after a divorce. Coincidence? I think not.

Of course, you also have to play family politics. You don't want to offend or upset anyone. "Well, I spent last Christmas with Dad, so this Christmas I should spend with Mom to be fair." Or when both parents invite you to Thanksgiving and you have to choose where you'll go. I've tried cloning myself, but it didn't work out too well. In that scenario, I try to come up with a hybrid solution. "Okay, I'll be with Dad for the actual Thanksgiving Day on Thursday but fly out the next day and spend the weekend with Mom."

Next, why do people fall out of love? What changes? I think the answer lies within their expectations. We often enter into a relationship expecting it to be a certain way, only to later become disappointed when it isn't close to what we pictured in our heads. And why not? This sounds very reasonable. When you meet someone and get to know them, you're buying into a concept. "What is the product they're selling me? Do I want this or not?" The only difference is that in this case, the product is an actual person and their personality. It's a transaction of emotional goods.

I know we don't like to view things in this way, since relationships are much more complex than a simple buying and selling transaction. But when someone buys into a person and things change down the road, it's only natural to be upset. "You pitched me X. I *liked* X. I thought I was buying X. Now you tell me it's actually Y? I didn't sign up for Y. I don't want Y. I'm selling Y back to you!"

Granted, people are not products. Unlike products, we evolve and constantly change over time. Therefore, the initial X when you first met someone will morph into many different letters, shapes, and sizes over a period of years. If we're constantly changing as people, and nothing ever stays the same, then how do two people remain invested in each other? Must they always morph together, and at the same pace? Adaptability is very important; in my experience, problems arise when one person remains static in their ways and seems incapable of evolving. Your needs change over time. What you needed from your partner five years ago is very different from what you need today. However, if your partner always remains static in their ways, then it's eventually going to be met with friction in the relationship.

There is one thing that never changes: your core values. Empathy, compassion, humor, intellect, positivity; these are the things you are actually buying into (or *should* be buying into). While everything else can change in a relationship, core values tend to shift very little, if at all, over time. At the end of the day, I believe if a couple's core values are well-aligned, then they have a much stronger chance of sticking together through thick and thin.

To address my previous question, "Why are we so bad at choosing?" I believe it's because more often than not, we're failing to choose a partner based on their core values. Rather, we tend to be focused on more of the "transactional" qualities: What do they bring to the table? What's their educational background? What's their family's background? What private clubs are they a part of, if any? What kind of job do they have? How much money do they make?

These are all the wrong questions. Instead, you should be asking yourself, "Is this person motivated? Are we aligned in the same core values? Do we appreciate the same things in life? Do we share similar outlooks?" These are much better indicators as to whether you'll have a happy marriage and relationship, rather than where someone went to school, what job they have, or what family they were born into.

Finally, I can't talk about divorce without at least mentioning the ultra-sensitive topic of prenuptials (or, for the more progressive, postnuptials). Let me be clear: I do not want to come across as insensitive to this issue. I certainly understand and empathize with the "opportunity cost" argument: "I sacrificed a career to help raise our child, therefore I deserve half of our money." But I can also see the other side of the debate: "Whatever we enter with we leave with." I happen to think there's a middle ground.

It's obviously hard to discuss these issues when you're in love, because it signifies there might be an end somewhere down the road, but I believe it's important to have *something* down in writing. Think of it like an insurance policy; this will never happen, so we have nothing to worry about, but just in case something *does* happen . . . I've seen many people's lives ruined because they didn't have something in writing. Every relationship dynamic is unique, and there are professionals who are far better equipped than I to provide an answer to this question. My advice: have a tough conversation with your loved one, seek the consultation of a professional, and never discuss it again.

In 2007, my mother remarried and moved to Minneapolis, Minnesota. Shortly thereafter, my father remarried and stayed in New York City. Watching both my parents marry new people is something I never thought I'd experience. Obviously, remarriage is not a new concept. But for a teenager, seeing your parents walk down the aisle—separately—is not something you expect to witness, nor is having to give a speech at your mom's and then your dad's wedding. But, hey, who cares about tradition these days? Here's my approach to this nontraditional, yet ever-more-common modern family life.

After divorce, new people come into your life. What, did you expect your parents to never find love again? This second time around, however, the circumstances are a little different and things feel a little more forced from the child's perspective. I have new parents? I have four parents now, you say? How does that work? Who do I listen to? And from whom do I solicit advice? All valid questions.

First off, it really depends on how old the child is and where in the developmental process they are when the parents get remarried. There's a huge difference between marrying someone with children under ten, for example, versus someone whose children are over eighteen. Then the question becomes how involved the stepparents are going to be in raising the child and imparting their wisdom and values. I would argue that a child under twelve or thirteen is going to be far more receptive to new parenting styles than a seventeen-year-old.

From a legal perspective, if all the children are above eighteen, then there are no custody requirements, no need to legally split time between parents. Fortunately, this was the case for my sister and me. Neither of my stepparents raised me from a young age, so there were and still are limitations to what I discuss with them. It's not that I don't respect their opinions or great life advice; on the contrary. It's just that they don't have the same connection with me and responsibility toward me as my birth parents. However, I'd like to give credit to all stepparents for trying their best to make an awkward situation, well . . . a little less awkward.

Which brings me to my next observation: adults who didn't have the experience of raising children act very differently than those who did. I know this might sound like an obvious statement, but it's something I've become much more sensitive to when being introduced to people of an older generation, including stepparents. If you've never raised kids of your own, you've simply never had to put someone else's interests ahead of yours. You've never had to put your own life goals on hold for someone else. This is an incredibly powerful, life-changing experience.

Stepparents can often operate under their own personal agendas. (As they should. I don't say this in a judgmental way. It's not necessarily a negative thing.) Stepparents are just people, like anyone else. And if anything, their allegiance is to their spouse and their own children . . . but not necessarily to their spouse's children. As a stepchild, you may need to occasionally remind yourself of this fact. Don't let it bother you when you think a stepparent acts in a way that is inconsistent with your own ideology. Take things with a grain of salt—chances are they care about you and are doing the best they know how in these strange new circumstances.

The situations I find most fascinating are when both pairs of parents and stepparents are forced into the same room together. This rarely happens; perhaps it's at a child's graduation or wedding. Do you need separate celebratory dinners? Which friends do you invite? Can the parents be in the same room as each other? How far apart do they need to sit? Will they even talk to each other? Here's the bottom line: who the hell am I to judge? I just want both of my parents to be happy. If each stepparent is capable of producing this, then isn't that enough? Can't I just be happy with that? If you so happen to like your stepparents, then great! But if not, so what? Personally, it's not like I have to be married to them or live with them. And is my own life and relationship so perfect? Who am I to criticize others? People need to worry a little less about other people's lives and a little more about their own. Focus on *your* happiness. That's my advice.

16

Everyone Is (Not) Doing It

I'VE BEEN CONCUSSED ON TWO SEPARATE OCCASIONS **IN MY LIFE.** The first was at fifteen years old, when an acquaintance sucker-punched me in the middle of a Manhattan street and I fell headfirst to the concrete. The second was at twenty-five, when someone decided it would be funny to push the birthday boy into the pool. I hit my head on the edge on the way into the water. Needless to say, both were scary scenarios. Fortunately, I made a full recovery both times, but not without some valuable and painful lessons in the process.

It was probably the scariest day of my life. I'll never forget the look on both my parents' faces, not sure if their son would ever be able to speak or be, well, normal again. It's difficult to describe the frustration of struggling to answer even the most basic questions: "What's your name? Where do you live? What school do you go to? Who is this person?" I knew the answers in my head, but I struggled to communicate them. I was in the hospital, unsure of how I got there or what had happened to me. I felt like an infant in an adult's body. I was only fifteen years old.

The next six months were a long and arduous road to recovery. I suffered from almost complete short-term memory loss, which made going to school even more difficult. It was an interesting phenomenon; I would ask

a question and get a response, and then ask the same question five minutes later. My friends would tell me, "Peter, you just asked that question." I was embarrassed and frustrated. My head felt cloudy for several months—I just couldn't get a firm grasp on anything, and I never felt truly present. I had minor bleeding in the brain but no hemorrhage, and my brain healed itself over time. After six months, and many MRIs and psychological tests, I had finally made a full recovery.

The details of the incident are quite fascinating, although, honestly, I don't have much interest in delving into them. The real irony of the whole thing is that when this happened, it was the very first time my parents trusted me to be on my own for the weekend without a sitter to watch over me while they were away. The kid who punched me was a relative of a very famous American financier who shares the same last name (hint). My father, despite being a corporate attorney, was not a particularly litigious man and decided not to sue the family for damages. We did, however, press charges, which got a detective involved in the case. Some might consider my father to have taken the high road, but I don't think so. If it were my kid who may have been permanently brain-damaged, I'd be suing the perpetrator for everything they had. I'd donate the money to my child as free college tuition later in life, since they're the one who would have to deal with the injury . . . but, hey, that's just me.

The second incident occurred at my twenty-fifth birthday party in Miami. Some drunk girl decided it would be hilarious to push me into the pool. What she failed to take into consideration was exactly where I was positioned relative to the edge of the pool, and I smacked my head on the way down. I didn't lose consciousness, and there was no bleeding this time around, but I was definitely concussed. I had been drinking heavily, which made the situation all the more dangerous.

Now that I was legal to drink, I was discovering firsthand just how real the pressure is to drink in social settings when you're in your early twenties. It's pretty incredible, actually; not only do friends make fun of you if you're not drinking, but you internalize those feelings and come to view drinking as obligatory. Even if you don't want to drink, you're so young that you don't know how to be yourself, so you just . . . drink. When you're young and immature, you become solely concerned with fitting in rather than standing out (in your early thirties, this reverses). It's easy to worry about what other people think of you—you simply lack the life experience to know any different.

Over the next few months, while I was attempting to recover from my concussion, I would frequently go out in social situations and be forced to drink even when I didn't want to. And, every time, this caused a weeklong hangover and a recovery setback, because my brain was sensitive and still trying to heal. But what was I supposed to do? Not live my life? Most adults, and certainly my parents, didn't understand at the time. And what's even more frustrating is that most people still wouldn't understand today. "Peter, just don't drink when you're with your friends." It's so easy to say that as a mature adult, but, if you can, try putting yourself in the shoes of a twenty-five-year-old. Your whole world is completely different. So much of your social life is based on drinking. Young people oftentimes don't know how to have fun if alcohol isn't involved. They have a hard time choosing their own health over wanting to fit in. The social forces are intense. And herein lies the true lesson of this chapter: don't allow yourself to be peer-pressured.

This is easier said than done. Often, young people are extremely concerned with being judged, especially at an age when everyone is more or less healthy. It can feel weird to stick out within your peer group—I get it! But, seriously, how much happier would everyone be if we actually got to be ourselves and didn't just do things because others thought we should? I've come to realize that you can't live your life according to what others think you should be doing. In fact, you can't live your life according to what even *you* think you should be doing. Forget the word "should." There is only you and the free-flow of life decisions. You must live your life organically and focus on being present. Remove any egoic version of yourself. Chasing this idea of who you think you should be will only ever lead to anguish and frustration. It's simply not sustainable. You are who you are. We are all flawed human beings. Own it, embrace it, and stop judging others and yourself. Just focus on trying to become a better human being instead. I promise, you'll be happier.

So, next time you're at a bar or out with friends and someone offers you a drink you don't want, just say, "Thanks for the offer, but I'm good," or, "Order me a club soda with lime." I do it often. Is it awkward at times? Perhaps. But I can tell you, 1) anyone who judges you for it is probably not someone you want to be close friends with, 2) your true friends will actually respect you more for staying true to yourself and showing discipline, 3) you'll probably make a better first impression on anyone you meet, because you won't be acting sloppy, and 4) you'll feel a whole lot happier for it (as will your wallet and head the next morning).

17

Your Fundamental Insecurity

IGREW UP GOING TO SUNDAY SCHOOL EVERY WEEKEND. I went to an episcopal high school called St. Paul's. My father was Christian, my mother Jewish. Yet somehow, despite (or because of?) all that, I ended up being an atheist. I was a philosophy minor in college and thoroughly enjoyed studying existentialism, including works such as *Being and Nothingness* by Jean-Paul Sartre. In this chapter, I'm going to examine what being atheist means, how to avoid pissing people off (or getting yourself killed), and exactly how I reached this conclusion. I'm hardly alone—millennials are becoming agnostic and atheist at a much faster rate than any previous generation. I think the more pertinent question to explore is: why are so many millennials giving up church?

Ah, religion! Are your antennae up yet? Ready to get emotional or combative if you don't 100 percent agree with me? It's a sensitive issue for many. Very rarely do you meet someone who says, "I don't have an opinion on religion"

(is that even an option?). And there's a very simple reason for this, besides the fact that it has cultural influences that date back thousands of years: It involves life and death. Literally.

Your position on this issue will influence your opinion on several other emotional and behavioral factors, such as whether or not there is an afterlife, whether you owe anything to a higher being, where you spend your time on Sundays, the kinds of people you might want to connect with, how you draw up values and principles, and even to some extent your political views (despite all efforts among our founding fathers to separate church and state in our founding documents). Religion is about as personal as it gets. So, let's take a deep breath in, relax, and for the moment try to put our "objective" hats on. It'll be okay. Ready?

First, I believe there's a huge difference between someone who is "atheist" versus someone who is "an atheist." I know, subtle difference, right? But "atheist," as an adjective, suggests an individual taking an active stance and being part of a larger team. "I'm X. And I stand here with my other X members as a show of force that we stand firmly together." Rather, saying, "I'm an atheist," as a noun, suggests, "I'm an X. I really don't give a shit if other people are part of X or not. I'm not part of any larger team." It's a much more solitary stance.

The point is, regardless of your religious beliefs (or lack thereof), no one likes a person who preaches or proselytizes, someone so closed-minded and insecure in their own beliefs that they feel the need to validate themselves by pushing them onto you and telling you what you should believe. How fucking childish is this behavior? I'm an atheist. However, I do not try to "convert" anyone or impose my views on people. Why not? Because I'm secure in my views and comfortable with the path I've chosen. That's why I don't feel the need to discuss it. To be honest, I don't even really think about it, except when I'm forced to by people who are less secure in their beliefs and therefore feel a need to challenge mine. So, rule number one . . . Don't preach.

Second, let me just explain my rationale (it's okay if you don't agree with it). At the end of the day, my view is that you do whatever you have to do to sleep better at night. I'm not judgmental, but I don't personally believe in organized religion (self-practiced religion is fine). Organized religion, in my humble opinion, has caused more harm than good. Millions of people have died in religious warfare over thousands of years. It's more divisive than it is communal. It prevents people from getting along with each other. Which leads me to the next question: What is the purpose of religion? Why does it exist?

I'm going to assume for the moment that if you're reading this, you don't literally believe Jesus Christ was an actual person, the son of God, and walked on water. If you do fall into this category, then I apologize in

126

advance because you're probably not going to like anything I'm about to say. However, if you believe that these stories were fables, and that religion was created by humans and shaped by societies over long periods of time, then read on.

The most practical purpose of religion has always been to provide society with a general moral guide. Be kind to thy neighbor. Don't kill. Don't cheat. Don't steal, etc. (I'm paraphrasing a bit.) Further, it can reinforce these values by creating a sense of community and providing physical property where its people can conglomerate (churches, temples, monasteries, mosques). Nothing wrong with that. But who said you can't believe these things *without* religion? Isn't it still possible to share those same moral principles without being a part of any specific religious hierarchy?

The second and much more potent way religion affects us concerns the afterlife, which brings me to what I call . . .

THE FUNDAMENTAL INSECURITY

We all have insecurities, (Except for YOU. You're perfect.) "Am I too chubby?" "Am I successful?" "What do people think of me?" "Is my nose too long?" These are all natural, normal human thoughts. They can vary widely, having to do with appearance, emotions, career, whatever. However, I believe that every person shares one common insecurity that's rooted deep to their core and subconsciously dominates all other insecurities: "Why are we here? And what happens to us when we die?" This is what I call the *fundamental insecurity*.

This is, for obvious reasons, a deeply troubling and uncomfortable question to ponder. I've spent thousands of hours trying to answer this question, through all my Sunday school teachings growing up, theology lessons at St. Paul's, and philosophy and psychology studies in college. The answer I've come up with (which predictably may not sit well with you) is the following: nothing. There is no actual "reason" we're here, and there's nothing that happens to us after we die. In time, all our accomplishments will be forgotten. Earth will naturally die out billions of years from now. And there is no "purpose" for us; we were just the lucky ones who got to be born and experience it all for a small nano-fraction of time.

I know, this is a scary idea. The notion that this might be it, that there is nothing after this, strikes a strong emotional reaction. As humans, we start to trigger a defense mechanism to deal with this cold, harsh reality. We start to rationalize and create other concepts. "No, this can't be it. Something lives on. Like our soul! Our soul MUST live on." Through our own mental defense mechanism (self-preservation, evolution, and our innate desire to survive), and in order to solve this "problem," religion was born. Religion solves this mental anguish by creating a concept of *afterlife*, either literally or figuratively, that puts our mind at ease so we can live a little easier.

The manifestation of religion and afterlife is given further credibility by its guiding moral principles and teachings, which make it an easier product to sell to society. But, make no mistake, the idea of afterlife and any values and teachings that religion provides technically have nothing to do with each other and should be considered mutually exclusive. Can you imagine if I could somehow disprove that there is a god or an afterlife? There would be mass hysteria, rioting, and chaos in society. People can't easily come to terms with this concept of finite versus infinite. It goes against all our body's evolutionary defenses. It creates a fundamental insecurity.

Let's take a deep breath. How are we doing? Ready to riot in the streets? Didn't think so.

Now that we've absorbed that information a bit, I feel the need to clarify further (since I've probably upset a few people). 1) In accordance with my principles and to be consistent, I again preface that these are my own beliefs, and I'm not telling anyone else to believe them. I respect any ideological differences of opinion we may have. You're entitled to believe anything you want to believe, free from judgment or persecution. 2) A common response I get to this is, "Well, Peter, if the meaning of life is nothing, then why don't we all just go kill ourselves?" This misinterprets my belief. Our life *does* have meaning; it's just that we have to supply the meaning ourselves for the duration of time we're still breathing.

There is no "higher" meaning or purpose for humanity, other than to enjoy life and all that it has to offer. You should take every advantage of this gift you've been given—and trust me, it is a gift. Many have never experienced it simply because they were never born. 3) Moreover, a funny thing happens the sooner you come to accept this fate: you actually appreciate life *more*. You come to understand the sheer finality of death and that we are so lucky to be alive. Realizing there's nothing after this makes you much more appreciative of life's special and ordinary little moments, because you're not holding out hope for something better down the road.

"But, Peter, if you don't believe in religion, where do you get your values from?"

Fair question.

My guiding principle comes simply from the Golden Rule (yes, I realize it's a traditionally Christian teaching). "Do unto others as you'd have them do unto you." Or you can subscribe to the inverse of that: "Don't do unto others as you wouldn't want done unto you." Either way, it's a pretty basic concept. Treat others the way you want to be treated—with kindness, respect, care, compassion, and love. I don't want to be hurt, so I try not to hurt other people. I don't want my stuff to be stolen, so I don't steal from others.

Here's the reality: my views are much less controversial among my peer group than among older generations. In fact, I would argue I'm in the majority rather than the minority of people my age—millennials. Many friends of mine share similar sentiments; they just choose not to be as vocal as I am. They may not necessarily be atheist, but they sure aren't going to church on Sundays. So, why are millennials giving up on more traditional, formal practices of religious institutions? Why is the church losing young people?

TWO THOUGHTS:

1. As we continue to progress as a society, younger people are finding it more difficult to buy into the archaic practices and beliefs of the church. (Is that the fault of young people? Or the fault of the church for not being able to adapt and stay relevant?)

2. Going to church isn't cool. It's not that younger people have given up on the idea of community (despite the urbanization of America and the increase of metropolitan living), it's just that they're seeking it in less traditional ways. With the advent of social media such as Facebook and Instagram, young people are seeking a sense of community through alternative methods, such as going to yoga together, meditation, group fitness classes, entrepreneurial meetups, etc. These channels provide the same sense of community fulfillment, but without the thousands of years of historical and emotional baggage and the barriers of church.

In closing, try to enjoy every moment life has to offer. Don't have regrets; you don't get another life. Try to live with compassion and love for yourself and others. Ultimately, do what makes you feel happy and fulfilled (assuming it's legal), don't intentionally cause harm to others, and don't let anyone get in your way, ever. Life is too damn short. Just appreciate the gift we've been given and soak it all in, no matter what you believe. Despite our differences, the truth is, we're all on the same ride.

18

The Immortal Game

IN THE FIRST HALF OF MY LIFE (BEFORE I DISCOVERED GIRLS), I WAS A NATIONALLY RANKED CHESS PLAYER AND FLEW AROUND THE COUNTRY COMPETING IN TOURNAMENTS. I even had a private chess coach (only in New York would such a thing exist) and spent a lot of time learning from the famous grandmaster Bruce Pandolfini (see the movie *Searching for Bobby Fisher*; Ben Kingsley plays the role of Bruce). I used to be embarrassed by this part of my life, but I've learned to appreciate its qualities and lessons. I think it's worth sharing my relationship with chess, and why I believe everyone should learn how to play.

As far as the eye can see, there are rows upon rows of chess tables and thousands of players, all smacking their clocks. Somewhere within the sea of kings, queens, and rooks, I'm waiting for my opponent to make his move, staring him down after 120 grueling minutes of play. I can feel the anxiety in the room as everyone watches . . . and waits.

I'm laser-focused. A bomb could go off and I wouldn't hear it. My heart has never beat so quickly before in my life. He has no chance; I've already mapped out the next four moves and analyzed every single one of his possibilities. *Don't mess this up, Pete. Don't touch the wrong piece*, I think. I know what's at stake, although I've never been in this territory before. I've

spent hundreds of hours practicing moves, analyzing positions and openings, and working with numerous coaches, and my family has invested thousands of dollars in private tutoring, all for this moment.

It's the seventh and final game of the 1999 National Elementary Chess Championships in Phoenix, Arizona. The end of a mind-scorching three-day weekend, and I'm currently sitting half a point behind the leader in my division. Granted, it's not the open division and therefore not the highest level of play, but the competition is still fierce. After drawing my first match, I proceeded to win the next five in a row. I'm now one win away from finishing with 6.5 out of 7 points, and for sure a top-five placement. I know my national ranking will soar if I can finish this off. This is what it must feel like to be Mariano Rivera of the New York Yankees, trying to get the final three outs to win the World Series. Or at least as close as I'll ever get to experiencing that kind of rush.

After twenty minutes of staring, my opponent finally makes his move. It's not a surprise—I already predicted he would make that move. He's not stupid, either. He knows he's stuck. Without hesitation, I move my knight.

"Checkmate," I say in a firm, quiet voice.

We shake hands, and I bring the official scoresheet to the judge's table, then proceed down the hall. I'll never forget the excitement rushing to my head during that walk. I'm about to announce what everyone is waiting to hear. "I won," I finally say. Cheers and yelling ensue, and I feel like I'm on top of Mount Everest. Later that evening, I'm presented with a trophy five feet tall—almost as tall as me. The hard work has paid off.

This is just one example of the many joys chess can bring. I understand that for most people, chess is typically associated with nerdy boys. And while this may be true to an extent, it's certainly not true of everyone. I'd like to challenge that notion and be an advocate of the idea that playing chess is cool, attractive, and teaches you lots of important skills. Most importantly, chess teaches you to critically analyze each position, looking at each moving piece in detail and at the entire range of possible scenarios. The game requires that you take a step back to look at the big picture in order to determine the most favorable outcome. "If I do X, then what will my opponent do in return as Y? And then what will I do after?" And so on and so forth, for multiple degrees into the future.

Also, you never want to be surprised by your opponent's move. Otherwise the entire thirty minutes you spent analyzing the position will go to waste, and you'll have to start all over again with the new data you've been presented. This forces you to be incredibly granular and detail-oriented; no move can be overlooked. And it teaches you the art of deception. *I'll make some weird move to my left, when really all I'm trying to do is take your attention away from the attack I'm building to my right to checkmate you.*

Lastly, another big chess and life lesson is to never play "hope chess," as in, "I hope my opponent will make this mistake so that I can exploit it." You learn to always *assume and expect* that your opponent will make the best move possible, in any situation. While it's always important to have an action plan, be ready to deviate from it at any moment. You can't react or make decisions based on hypothetical future scenarios that don't currently exist; you must live in the now and react to the current situation at hand. You learn to deal with the cards you've been dealt and make the most of it.

All the aforementioned lessons are in addition to the more obvious benefits of playing chess, such as learning how to compete, how to lose gracefully, how to deal with failure, and how to get back up on your feet and try again and again . . . and again.

Of course, I'm not the only person who feels this way about chess. About fifteen years ago, I heard that several private schools in New York City had started incorporating a forty-five-minute mandatory chess class into their curriculum. I hope many other schools have since followed this trend.

Chess isn't just a game, either. If anything, it's the game of life, teaching you how to act with poise and intelligence in every situation that comes your way. When you enter a new company at the ground floor, you're the pawn, and the CEO is the king. How do you think they made it to that position? Probably through sheer hard work and determination. Do you want to get there someday? Then play the game; start making the right moves. All of life is a chess board, but you need to decide which piece you want to be.

I used to be embarrassed mentioning my chess history to girls, but that's because I was at an age where there existed a lot of immaturity and stereotypes. After growing out of that phase and maturing into my early thirties, I've since discovered that any quality woman (or man) will find this attractive and appealing.

So, ladies and gentlemen, it's never too late to start playing chess. I encourage you to teach your kids the game early on, as it will pay many dividends later in life. Never be afraid to tell others you play chess. In fact, my history in the game has led to some awesome dates and interesting conversations.

One of the millennial generation's most admirable values is that they are overwhelmingly more likely to spend money on experiences than on stuff

Advent

urous Millennial

19

Eye of a Hurricane

IN THE FALL OF 2005, THREE HURRICANES IMPACTED SOUTHERN FLORIDA WITHIN A SHORT TIME SPAN: RITA, WILMA, AND KATRINA. While much attention is given to Katrina's catastrophic impact on New Orleans, few people remember that it actually first made landfall directly over Miami-Dade County (granted, it was a weaker storm before it strengthened in the Gulf). I was a freshman at the University of Miami, and it was only the first week of classes when Katrina struck. I was in the middle of rushing different fraternities and didn't want to be stuck in the freshman dorms during mandatory "campus lockdown" for several days, so I decided to go off campus the night before Katrina struck and stay in the home of a fraternity member. This is my survival story of the events that unfolded (and what *not* to do).

AUGUST 25, 2005, 5:30 A.M.
CORAL GABLES, FLORIDA

"Pete, wake up! Wake up!"

It's Jordy, and he's shaking me.

"Jordy, I'm still sleeping," I moan. "What's wrong?" I think I'm still drunk.

"You want to go on an adventure?"

I sit up, intrigued. "What do you mean, *adventure*?"

"I think I left the doors open and unlocked in the chapter house. It might flood. I'm the house manager, and it's my responsibility to make sure everything's okay. I need to walk over there. Things are deteriorating fast."

"Fuck, man." I rub my eyes and glance out the window. "How far is it?" It's dark and windy outside. Looks like hell.

"About half a mile."

"Fuck." I take a deep breath and pretend to make some mental risk calculations in my head. "Let's do it. But we need to go *now*."

I quickly gather my belongings spread across the floor. There's a group of us staying in the house, and we had decided to play drinking games the night before the hurricane hit. I probably only slept for two or three hours.

As I step outside, I can't believe what I see. It looks completely apocalyptic, as if all humankind has been wiped off the earth in some cheap horror movie. Daylight's breaking, but there are no signs of life: no human activity, no cars on the street, no parked cars on the roads. Everything's boarded up. All we can hear is the incredibly loud howling of the wind against the buildings, like screaming.

As we start to walk west on Ponce de Leon Boulevard, the outer eye of Katrina passes right over us. The wind is so strong beating against our bodies that it takes five times the ordinary effort just to put one foot in front of the other and step forward. Winds are gusting up to 80 miles per hour, leaves, dust, and other particles are whipping around in the air and hitting our skin like ice pellets. I have to put my hands in front of my face and eyes to shield them from the pain.

I lean 45 degrees forward, as if I'm intentionally trying to fall forward, and the wind is so powerful it forces me back upright. To make matters worse (as if things aren't dangerous enough), there are physical hazards all over the place; downed tree branches and palm trees whipping around, power lines and traffic lights in the middle of the roadway, and lots of flying garbage. After a few hundred feet, we're physically and mentally drained.

"JORDY!" I scream. He can barely hear me. I start waving my hands in large sweeping motions and pointing to my right. "SHELTER. WE NEED SHELTER!" I spot a stairwell and crevice sandwiched between two larger buildings where we can hide to catch our breath. We rush inside, shivering.

"That's pretty intense out there," Jordy says through heavy breathing.

I'm beginning to regret my decision to come along on this "adventure" as I finally begin to understand why the meteorologists on television make such a big deal about staying indoors during a hurricane. I'm feeling overwhelmed by the thought that we still have a long distance to go. Can we make it? At this point, there truly is no turning back. All I can focus on is the debris and incredible wind tunnels unfolding in front of me.

"All right. Let's keep going," I say in a low voice, terrified.

We continue our trek up the road, dodging more hazards along the way. I glance at my watch: 7:30 a.m. We've been battling the elements for an hour and a half. Given that we're near the eye of the hurricane, there's no rain. As we finally near the end of the road and get closer to the fraternity house, I see the first living thing I've seen all morning: a cop car coming toward us.

"WHAT ARE YOU GUYS DOING?" the officer yells from his rolled down window, alarmed by our stupidity, which, frankly, alarms me, too. Without even giving us a chance to answer, he yells, "GET INSIDE IMMEDIATELY. IT IS TOO DANGEROUS TO BE OUTSIDE!" and speeds off in his patrol car. Upon reflection, it would have been nice of him to offer us a ride. But no such offer is given.

We're *so* close. I can see the finish line. Then, just 200 yards from the house, the first eye wall hits us . . . hard. Suddenly, rain starts pouring down like nothing I've ever experienced before. Giant raindrops the size of golf balls. Our clothes are instantly drenched, and loud thunder cracks overhead. Now we really begin to panic. With all the energy we can muster, we start to run.

Fortunately, there isn't too much damage to the house. Jordy wasn't lying; the front doors are swung wide open. The ground floor has some mild flooding, and some of the windows are shattered, allowing water to soak the carpets. I take a hot shower, help put some towels and other barriers against the openings, and finally find an empty bed to lie down in. There'll be plenty of time later to second-guess my poor decision-making, but in the moment I'm thinking, *I just walked through the eye of a hurricane and survived. Not too many people can say that.* Little did I know that Katrina would go on to strengthen and become the costliest and deadliest hurricane ever recorded in the Atlantic, with 1,833 fatalities and $108 billion of damage.

What's the lesson in all this, you ask? Simple. Don't do what I did. Hurricanes are no joke.

20

The Honey Hunters

ON MAY 29, 2008, MY MOTHER AND I WENT ON AN ADVENTURE IN TANZANIA TO DISCOVER THE NOMADIC AFRICAN "HADZABE" TRIBE. Far more remote and lesser known than the popular "Maasai," the Hadzabe live in complete isolation from the rest of the world (and due to their nomadic lifestyle, are much harder to find). I witnessed something that day that I didn't think was humanly possible.

For a few years following my parents' divorce, my mother took my sister and me on separate trips to a place of our choosing. My sister typically selected beach destinations like St. Barthélemy, whereas I preferred Indiana Jones-type adventures. I want to wander off the beaten path, somewhere other than Paris or Rome or all the other places Americans typically go.

For our first trip, I went to the travel section at Barnes and Noble and looked in books for the most exotic-sounding place I could find. The first destination I decided upon was Tunisia. I had never heard of Tunisia, none of my friends had ever talked about Tunisia, and I didn't know anyone who had been there. It also happened to be where *Star Wars* was filmed, and some of the sets from the 1970s were still intact. Sounded like a great place! Each year that's how I chose our destination. My mother has been a trooper—we've traveled to Tunisia, Bhutan, Egypt, and Jordan, among others.

In May of 2008, Mom had the idea to go on a safari, so we set off to Tanzania in East Africa. While we were in Tanzania, we stayed in a number

of places that ranged from the uniquely beautiful Ngorongoro Crater Lodge to the upscale Grumeti Serengeti Tented Camp. I'll never forget sleeping in that camp. At the Grumeti, we were warned not to go outside our tent in the middle of the night because there might be hippos. Little-known fact: hippos cause more human deaths each year than any other African animal. They're one of the most dangerous animals, and extremely territorial.

In the middle of the night, I heard loud breathing and snoring—a goddamn hippo was lying down about two feet outside our tent. The only thing separating it from us was a thin veil of fabric. I was scared shitless. I didn't want to move lest I wake him up, so I laid perfectly still all night. Thankfully, by the time we got up the next morning, he was gone.

We planned the trip to coincide with the "Great Migration," in which the Serengeti wildebeest move north in search of water and fresh areas to graze. Accompanied by a travel guide and riding in a Jeep, Mom and I found ourselves—the only humans anywhere nearby—in the midst of one of the main herds. The sight was spectacular. Swarming on all sides were tens of thousands of moving animals as far as the eye could see. I kept hoping we wouldn't piss them off or disturb them for any reason.

We then decided we wanted to meet one of the local Tanzanian tribes. The Maasai tribe is known to be friendly to tourists, and plenty of guides and tour companies call on them to host international visitors. But the Maasai are like the Times Square of Tanzanian tribal attractions. They're local, but they're huge. I wanted to experience something unique, so we set off on a mission to locate the Hadzabe instead.

The Hadzabe (also called the Hadza) are one of the oldest lineages of the human race, and they live in complete seclusion from the rest of the population. Though they have lost access to vast amounts of land, they still live the same hunter-gatherer lifestyle of their ancestors. They're the last remaining tribe to hunt within the Serengeti for survival.

I've always been someone to take risks because I want to have atypical life experiences. That's my basic ethos. I want to do things other people may be too scared to do. There's a difference between reckless risk and calculated risk, of course. I wouldn't do something like square off with a hippo, for example. And it's not like I was seeking an adventure with the drug lords of the Congo. The Hadzabe are quite remote, but visiting them would be relatively safe.

Or so I thought.

We left the wildebeest and embarked on a lengthy trek deep into the African bush. The Hadzabe are nomadic and roam the area around Lake Eyasi in northern Tanzania, which meant they were difficult to find. After three or four hours of searching, we came upon a multifamily dwelling, and our guide helped us communicate with them. The Hadzabe language is very primal and includes clicking sounds for consonants. The conversation also included quite a few hand gestures and lots of pointing. Our guide barely spoke their dialect, but without him we would have been entirely lost.

The men, simply covered in fabric togas or loose T-shirts, were about to head out for their daily hunt and invited me to join them. I hesitantly agreed, having no idea what I was signing up for. My mother stayed behind with the women to perform "womanly" duties, like cleaning and foraging for berries and such—when in Africa, do as the Africans do.

The hunters handed me a wooden bow and arrow carved from a tree branch. The guide, translating from the Hadzabe, asked, "You know how to shoot, right?"

"Of course. No problem," I said.

Now, I'm not trying to come off sounding uncultured or having had an overly sheltered upbringing in New York City. I went to a sleepaway camp and took archery lessons. I went on multi-week canoe trips through the Canadian wilderness. I even spent a summer living on Ometepe Island in Nicaragua. So, I've been out in the world. But when an African tribesman offers you a hand-hewn bow and arrow, what are you going to say? "No, sorry, that's illegal in Central Park," or, "No, sorry, we don't have those on Madison Avenue"? Right.

What the fuck was I supposed to do with this bow and arrow? Actually kill a wild animal in the Serengeti? What if I missed, and the animal got pissed off? Was Mr. Robin Hood over there in his toga going to save me at the last minute while a moving target charged 30 miles per hour right toward me? I don't think so. The whole scenario felt like a scene from a Billy Crystal comedy—except there was nothing funny or fake on this set.

So off we went into the bushes of the Serengeti, me all the while just hoping I would make it back alive. I wasn't even sure what I was supposed to be looking for or aiming at. All I kept thinking was, *Guys, I hope I'm not plan A. I hope you're not depending on this white kid from Manhattan to catch your dinner.*

Just then, the men stopped abruptly and pointed toward some branches above us, and next thing I knew several arrows flew through the air faster than I could look up. I wondered what the hell they were shooting at—a bird? A fowl of some sort? They missed and kept walking. I followed closely behind. After a few dozen yards, they stopped again. This time I clearly saw what they were targeting: a huge wild boar was grazing about twenty feet directly in front of us. I tried to remember some pages from my sixth-grade science book, frustrated that my memory was failing me, but I was pretty positive these were dangerous animals.

The Hadzabe moved very softly, crouched low to the ground. *This is it*, I thought. *This is how my life comes to an end, with a fucking boar in Africa.*

Parachute fails to open during skydiving? Heart attack during sex? Nope. A wild boar thrusting its tusk up my ass.

The hunters took aim, raising their bows and pointing their arrows right at the beast.

WHOOOOSH. The arrows soared toward the animal, but it rushed off in a fury in the opposite direction. I felt my heart skip a beat before returning to normal. With only a few arrows remaining and a disappointed look on their faces, the Hadzabe started to trek back toward their home camp. Are they just not going to eat today? I wondered. The stark reality settled in that these tribesmen couldn't just go to their local grocery store; they really depended on their daily catch for survival. It was a slow and quiet walk back. No words were exchanged. I continued to feel sad but also appreciative of how easy my own access to food is every day. I don't have to face down wild animals just to have lunch. I don't have to risk my life to provide food for myself and my family.

As we approached their camp, one of the tribesmen became very animated. He started making a lot of noise and jumping frantically. A flurry of communication transpired among them—clearly, they were excited about something. They pointed to a tree up ahead. Another animal, perhaps? I hoped it wasn't an elephant this time. I couldn't see anything on the tree, except for a little sliver of an opening cut into the trunk, way up toward the top, about twenty feet off the ground.

The Hadzabe quickly grabbed a few twigs and rubbed them together on a knife, almost instantly creating a small fire. Clearly, they had done this before. I was still confused as to what they were targeting. One of the tribesmen gathered a few pieces of burning bark in his hand and proceeded to climb the tree. He placed the smoking bark into the hole, and suddenly, 10,000 African bees raced out of the hole in a mad swarm. He reached his right arm into the hole and began to pull out giant, fresh chunks of honeycomb.

I was traumatized by the sight of this tribesman barely clothed in a loose, open shirt and covered with bees up and down the side of his body. These bees were no joke—these were African bees. I felt nauseous watching this unfold; I had never seen anything like it in my life.

The hunter started dropping the honeycomb down to his friends below. By this point, I had run backward about 200 yards. I'm terrified of just one bee, let alone 10,000. After a good ten minutes of waiting like a baby, I noticed the swarm calm down a bit and begin returning to their hive, and I finally caught back up with the men.

"Hey, guys! What'd I miss?"

The tribesmen were covered in stings. Later I learned that honey is an energy-rich, calorie-dense staple of the Hadzabe diet, so perhaps these guys are immune to the bee stings. Their people have been hunting honeycomb for thousands of years. But I'm pretty sure anyone else might have been killed, or at the very least would have needed emergency medical attention.

One of the men handed me a sample of the honeycomb. Imagine the sweetest, most incredibly rich honey you've ever tasted in your life and double it. It was so intense it made me sick to my stomach. But the starving tribesmen scarfed it down, practically inhaling it— I had never seen anyone eat so fast. This was likely their single source of nutrition, at least for that day.

I helped carry the remaining chunks of honeycomb back to their tribe for the women to enjoy, and rejoined my mother. We then took part in some song and dance, and the tribe gave us some trinkets and offerings before we departed back to our hotel in the Jeep.

A typical Tuesday in the Serengeti for these guys was one of the most unforgettable experiences I've ever had. But that's the way I love to live— daring myself to embrace experiences that challenge me.

The Hadzabe tribe has for generations created a simple life for themselves without any technology or dependency on other people. Though I'm grateful I can pick up dinner without chasing it down and killing it, I admire the self-sufficiency of this group who showed me you really can have a full life with so much less than Americans think they need.

As for my daily proximity to wildlife, I think I'll stick with the tiger moms, the primates of Park Avenue, and the wolves of Wall Street.

21

Cheering from the Sidelines

THERE ARE CERTAIN HISTORIC MOMENTS THAT YOU'RE LUCKY TO WITNESS. Rarely, however, can you claim to have any sort of direct influence on an historic event. On Sunday, August 5, 2012, at approximately 9:50 p.m. local time inside Olympic Stadium in London, American sprinter Justin Gatlin won the bronze medal in the 100-meter final competing against Usain Bolt. I will never forget the three words he whispered in my ear when it was over.

2 HOURS EARLIER
OLYMPIC STADIUM, LONDON, 7:42 P.M.
MEN'S 100-METER SEMIFINAL
ATTENDANCE: 80,000

"Come on, Justin!"

My mom and I are perfectly situated in the front row adjacent to the starting line. We watch as the different athletes go through their peculiar starting rituals: shaking their feet, making hand gestures to the camera, kissing the golden chain around their neck. It's a fierce semifinal heat; some of the top competitors include Asafa Powell of Jamaica, Churandy Martina of the Netherlands, Keston Bledman of Trinidad and Tobago, and Justin Gatlin of the United States, among a few others. The top three finishers will advance to the finals later this evening.

We're screaming at the top of our lungs, wearing official Team U.S.A. apparel and waving a mini American flag. Justin puts his head up and looks in our general direction. As far as I'm concerned, we're just two spectators among a crowd of 80,000 people, like everyone else. The noise and buzz in the stadium are so loud, I doubt he can even hear us cheering for him. My mom really hit a home run securing us these amazing seats.

Things start to settle down and get quiet.

Official Announcer: "On your marks."

The runners put their feet on the starting blocks, lower their bodies into the starting stance, and put their heads down. "Set."

The stadium goes silent.

BANG. The gun explodes, and the runners blaze out of their positions down the track. In under ten seconds they travel the distance of an entire football field. Before I can blink an eye, the race is over. Everyone is so fast, it's almost impossible to tell who won. We anxiously await the results on the jumbotron:

[#1 USA   GATLIN   9.82]
[#2 NED   MARTINA   9.91]
[#3 JAM   POWELL   9.94]

9.82 seconds! Not only did Justin Gatlin just secure a spot in the finals, but, more amazingly, he just ran the fastest recorded semifinal time in history. Shortly after the race, and unbeknownst to my mother and me at the time, Gatlin, on the verge of tears, conducted a very emotional TV interview with NBC:

"A lot of emotion here at the end of this semifinal," the host said, shoving a microphone at Gatlin. "Tell me about it."

"You know." He paused for what seemed like a very long time. "It's not about me. It's not about the next runner next to me or my teammates. It's about America. It's about what's on my chest, so I came out to do that. I felt okay. Once I saw the American flags right next to the starting blocks, people cheering for me, I did it for them."

Two Hours Later

100 Meter Finals

9:45 p.m. The stadium crowd is roaring as Usain Bolt walks into the arena. His 6' 5" physique and dominating presence can be felt reverberating throughout the entire crowd. Following close behind him are some other major forces of human nature: Yohan Blake and Asafa Powell of Jamaica; Tyson Gay, Justin Gatlin, and Ryan Bailey of the United States; Churandy Martina of the Netherlands; and Richard Thompson of Trinidad and Tobago. This is major firepower.

They line up to the starting blocks. The TV cameras are pointing on them. Millions of people are watching all over the world. Now my mom and I are really getting loud. "LET'S GO U.S.A! LET'S GO, JUSTIN!" The crowd noise is at a buzz, like an angry nest of African bees.

"On your marks."

The athletes once again get into their starting stance. The entire stadium quickly falls silent.

"Set." I can hear my breath inside my chest. I wonder if the runners can hear theirs.

BANG. The runners leap in a blazing fury and sprint down the track. Gatlin pulls to an early lead, but Bolt quickly starts to outpace him. Bolt closes the gap between them, and with a little bit of track remaining he gets out in front. They bow their heads at the last second, as sprinters customarily do at the finish line. It's very close. The results immediately appear on the jumbotron:

[#1 JAM USAIN BOLT   OR 9.63]
[#2 JAM YOHAN BLAKE   9.75]
[#3 USA JUSTIN GATLIN   9.79]
[#4 USA TYSON GAY   9.80]

The crowd is roaring once again. Bolt just set a new Olympic record for running a time of 9.63 seconds. Of course, he was the heavy favorite entering the race. Gatlin, however, just barely beat his teammate Tyson Gay by 1/100 of a second to earn the bronze medal.

The athletes are near the finish line taking photos and posing for the media while draped in their respective country's flags. My mother and I are on the opposite end near the starting line, watching the celebration unfold, along with thousands of other spectators, in complete awe. We're thrilled that an American won a medal. No easy feat, by any means.

To our surprise, Gatlin suddenly breaks away from Usain Bolt and Yohan Blake and starts walking back toward our general direction. Is he going to thank a parent standing in the crowd? Or maybe his longtime coach? Or just an old friend? I don't see him stopping. This is very peculiar. He keeps walking toward the starting line. He has a very determined look on his face. I take my digital camera out of my pocket; I may be able to catch a really close photo of him as he walks by! Incredible.

He's walking closer and closer in a straight line. It almost appears as if he's coming right toward . . . us? Who am I standing next to, I wonder? It must be someone very important to him. Gatlin is now less than five feet from where we're standing, and he keeps walking closer. Before I even realize what's happening, Justin Gatlin walks right up to me, drapes his arms with the American flag over my shoulders and gives me a hug. Very emotionally, he says into my ear, "You empowered me." He continues to hold me for twenty to thirty seconds, silent, then hugs my mother. To this day, I can't even remember if I was able to muster up any words for a reply.

At that very instant, a press photographer was standing on the track and caught this special moment. I'm still not sure why my mother and I were deserving of that. Talk about being in the right place at the right time. I'm just happy Justin won a medal, and I'm proud of Team U.S.A. for their incredible triumph and perseverance. I'm so humbled and thrilled that I could, to any extent possible, play a motivational role in helping an athlete compete at their best level. I don't accept any credit for that day; that, of course, all belongs to Justin. I am, however, very proud of my country and happy I could provide a small contribution. What's the lesson here? Small words can make a big difference. You have the potential to make a larger impact on someone's life than you realize, by simply showing support and cheering them on. Go U.S.A.!

22

Camp Montauk

IN THE SUMMER OF 2018, TWO CLOSE FRIENDS AND I DECIDED TO ORGANIZE A SLEEPAWAY CAMP FOR ADULTS IN MONTAUK, NEW YORK. We had over 350 friends stay over the course of the summer and branded it "Camp Montauk." The theme of the summer was "All Positivity, All the Time." The goal was simple: to unite different groups of friends and surround ourselves with positive, supportive people. It was not for monetary gain. I learned a lot of insights into the millennial generation that are worth sharing.

For those who are unaware, Montauk is a part of the "Hamptons," all the way at the very eastern end of Long Island. It has humble roots as a local fisherman and surfer town with a bohemian, laid-back pace. Sometimes branded as "the end of the world" because there's no farther east you can physically go, Montauk has a different reputation from other parts of the Hamptons. However, that all started to change several years ago.

For young New Yorkers living in Manhattan, it became primarily a summer party community due to more relaxed local laws and less "stuffiness" compared to the rest of the Hamptons. For the locals who actually lived there year-round, this became a living nightmare. The town of Montauk would jump from an estimated 20,000 residents to a whopping 150,000 for three months from June to August. It simply didn't have the infrastructure to support that kind of rapid growth.

On the flip side, property values quadrupled. Modest people who enjoyed a certain way of life now had an incredibly powerful asset that they never had before: their house. A standard three-bedroom home could rent for $50,000 to $60,000 a summer without a pool (add another $20,000 for that option). These figures are staggering, considering it's for only three months a year. Because Montauk became too expensive for 99 percent of young people, they naturally (and against code) started to subdivide. "Sharehouses," as they've come to be known, have actually been going on since the 1970s as a way for young people to meet and have fun without the jurisdiction of their parents' rules. My parents actually met at a sharehouse party in Westhampton in the mid 1970s.

Our house was going to be different. It was going to be run professionally, not like a traditional sharehouse. We came up with the idea to make it feel like a sleepaway camp when you were a kid, with bunks, cabins, and organized activities. We found a large, unique property tucked away in the woods with a pool, hot tub, hiking trails, and a hill in the backyard. We added giant fifteen-foot unicorn and peacock inflatables, a 100-foot slip and slide, and other fun Neverland-style games. We branded it "Camp Montauk."

We originally intended to have ten to twenty people participate in the house over the course of the summer. But word quickly got around, and referrals exploded beyond what we'd anticipated. We had over 350 people sign up (15 weekends x avg. 24 people per weekend = 360). It was a huge risk—out-of-pocket expenses, legal issues, risk of injury, etc. All it takes is one person to ruin the whole operation. But after running a large restaurant in Manhattan, I was mentally and physically prepared (or so I thought) for such a challenge and felt that the reward of uniting different groups of friends and having insane amounts of fun outweighed the risk. I can understand if most others would disagree and feel differently. You would have to be a little crazy to agree with me. Or just have an incredibly high tolerance for risk (which I do). More impressively, through clever marketing such as weekly newsletters and hosting a series of meet and greets at local bars and venues in the city, I single-handedly raised over $120,000 within a four-month period to pay for the house.

We had strict rules. This wasn't going to be *Animal House*. Over 70 percent of people signing up were women; therefore, it was imperative to create a safe environment where women felt comfortable all the time, and people of all different backgrounds and lifestyles could enjoy the space together. This was no easy task, especially given some of the strong New York personalities involved.

You're probably wondering: "Did you deal with any issues, Peter?"

Yes, all the time. I was constantly de-escalating situations. And I have some interesting private stories that could fill an entire book in itself. Most issues were minor, although we did have some major ones. Opening weekend, Memorial Day, I was at a wedding in Portugal and traveled sixteen hours straight in order to get to Montauk Sunday evening. I was so exhausted I went straight to bed, only to wake up Monday morning to find out someone staying in the house that weekend had made a sexual assault allegation. Fortunately, no one pressed charges; it seemed both people were drunk at the time. Regardless, we quickly installed security cameras in the house and asked both parties not to return.

Another scary incident was when our friend was high on drugs and/or alcohol and thought he could "fly" by jumping off the side railing seven feet off the ground, landing straight onto the dirt. I thought for sure he was going to be paralyzed, but he miraculously walked it off. Drugs became an issue, and we had to disinvite some friends from returning because they were supplying and doing drugs in open common spaces.

I don't enjoy being the "fun police," but I was responsible for everything that happened in the house. It was my name on the lease. All things considered, however, it was a huge success. People were overwhelmingly appreciative of the experience we had created, and campers would often say to me, "This is the best house I've ever been a part of." We had promised people the "greatest summer" of their lives, and I can confidently say we delivered. It's hard for me to go places in New York City now without running into some former camper.

More importantly, all fun and games aside, I learned some interesting insights into my generation, millennials.

01

MILLENNIALS TEND TO LIVE IN EXTREMES

Maybe it's the added pressures and stresses of living in such a large metropolitan city such as New York. But I call B.S. on that. I simply don't understand how you can go from living such a structured, regimented work life Monday through Friday, only to party all day and night with no sleep on weekends. But maybe that's what they consider balance.

02

MILLENNIALS OFTEN FORM ALTER EGOS

Interestingly, there would be people who were introverted and quiet in their daily life who became the extreme opposite (mostly when alcohol was involved). I just don't understand this. Where is this coming from? There aren't any excuses. It's not as if an alien life form temporarily took control of your body. This is still coming from *you*. Why is it so difficult to remain consistent in personality and temperament?

03

IF YOU GIVE SOMEONE AN INCH, THEY WANT A MILE

I would often go out of my way to do something nice for someone even though I didn't have to. Sometimes, however, people would take advantage. The moment I demonstrated that I was willing to go above and beyond, certain folks wanted that to be the norm. They *expected* it.

04

WOMEN WILL NOT TOUCH A PLUNGER

Under any circumstance. Nor will they ever admit to clogging a toilet.

05

GIRLS, SURPRISINGLY, ARE MESSIER THAN GUYS

Not more unsanitary. Girls by far take better care of their bodies and themselves, generally speaking. But I can't tell you how often a girl would eat a bowl of cereal and simply leave it there, expecting that it would be magically taken away by the phantom housekeeper.

06

GUYS ARE MORE DIFFICULT TO LIVE WITH THAN GIRLS

Now I understand what girls have to put up with. Guys are more stubborn, hardheaded, and particular about certain living conditions or sleeping arrangements, whereas girls are more adaptive, flexible, and appreciative. Guys would often give off an attitude of, "This is my way of doing things, and you need to get on board with it." Many times, I caught myself thinking, "Am I that difficult to deal with? I certainly hope not."

Some lasting advice from
one generation to another

Instru

ctive **Millennial**

23

How to Crush College

THIS CHAPTER IS TARGETED MORE TOWARD GENERATION Z, THE GENERATION AFTER MILLENNIALS, SINCE MOST MILLENNIALS HAVE ALREADY GONE TO COLLEGE. I attended the University of Miami (in Florida, not Ohio) from 2005 to 2009, and was both the social chair of a fraternity, as well as voted "Dream Man" of a sorority. I learned some interesting things along the way. It certainly wasn't your typical college experience, and I definitely focused a little more on social activities than studying, but I have absolutely zero regrets.

I hear a lot of people express regret regarding their college years. "I wish I had traveled abroad," they say. "I wish I hadn't had a boyfriend the entire time." "I wish I'd been more involved in campus organizations." What have I *never* heard someone say before? "I wish I'd spent more time in the library."

Don't get me wrong; college is definitely a time to learn, grow emotionally, and study. But there is always graduate school as an option to further your education. More than anything else, college is a time to grow as an adult, learn how to interact with people outside of your high school bubble, and experience new things (unless you attend an Ivy League school; then the pressure is a bit different). In other words, the whole point is to become a well-rounded human being. The worst thing you can do is leave college with regrets. Leave it all out there on the table, and don't ever look back! Here are some things I did to maximize my college experience.

CHOOSING THE RIGHT CAMPUS

Sometimes when you've had too much of something all your life, you reach for the exact opposite to balance it out. I spent my entire upbringing in the northeast and went to high school in freezing Concord, New Hampshire, where some days wind chill temperatures hit negative 20 degrees Fahrenheit. When it was time to choose where I wanted to go to college, I immediately focused on Florida and California. The University of Miami became my school. While it may not have necessarily been the "best" school I could have gone to, I could see myself thriving there.

Lesson one: don't go to the biggest "brand-name" school you can get into just because your parents or college advisors are pushing you in that direction. If you don't like the experience, it'll be a total waste. Also, I'm always surprised by other people's reactions when I tell them I grew up in New York yet went to school in Miami. Since when did it become a rule that you must go to college near where you grew up? I'm not trying to sound naïve; I understand that for many people, in-state tuition costs play a major role in their decision. But I think it has more to do with a tradition in this country to remain close to one's family. You have your entire life to be close to your family. Why not take advantage of the four years you've been given to explore a new part of the country and go outside your comfort zone? There are plenty of scholarship opportunities available, and you can always return home afterward.

A lot of people ask me if I went abroad while I was in college. Abroad? I was abroad. I lived right near Calle Ocho in Little Havana! As far as I'm concerned, I was in Cuba. I was in a whole new world; I felt very distant from the manicured streets of Madison Avenue in Manhattan. It was the best decision I could have made. I sorely needed a bit of worldly perspective.

So, be adventurous with your college decision. Your parents will be okay, I promise.

GREEK LIFE

I had the privilege of being a founding father of a new chapter for my fraternity, Beta Theta Pi, and later serving as social chair. Since graduating, I've continued to volunteer at the national level. Amid all the negative attention fraternities receive and the constant scrutiny by the media regarding hazing and other dangerous stuff, I feel it's important to explain why I believe in fraternities, and why I wouldn't be the person I am today without that experience. But I want to cut through all the PR nonsense and get straight to the point. Here's what joining a fraternity really teaches you: leadership, democracy, and failure. It's very unique to be awarded positions of responsibility at such an early age.

In a fraternity (or any organization, for that matter), you have the opportunity to earn a leadership position and be responsible for the wellbeing of 50+ other students. Not every choice on your plate will be an easy one, and more often than not you're going to be faced with difficult moral decisions of choosing what's in the best interest of the organization versus what's best for your friends. You'll be forced to lead by example. And, like in any democratic society, not everything you want is going to be voted in your favor.

A fraternity will force you to learn how to compromise, pick your battles wisely, and put others' interests ahead of your own. It will teach you that five heads together are stronger than one, and that sometimes you'll have to swallow your pride, hide your ego, and support other people's ideas, even if you ideologically disagree with them. More importantly, fraternities provide a safe ecosystem in which to make mistakes and learn from them before entering the "real world," where similar mental mistakes could prove much costlier. Yes, there is some stupid hazing stuff, and fraternities are working hard to disavow these activities nationwide. But the pros of Greek life far outweigh the cons. I wouldn't be the person I am today without it.

Do I have any regrets? Well, one. I should have run for student body president. I did the math, and due to low turnout, the winning candidate usually averages only 300-400 votes. I figure based on name recognition alone, plus votes from my entire fraternity and Tri Delta, I could easily have accumulated that number (and enacted some serious changes). But I wasn't thinking that big at the time. If you think big, then big things can happen. But if you think small, I guarantee you will achieve small results.

$\boxed{24}$

Business School and the Value of a Degree

"YOU'RE PAYING FOR CONNECTIONS." I HEAR THIS STATEMENT A LOT. I attended Babson F.W. Olin School of Business to study entrepreneurship from 2012-2014. As I reflect on my experience, I realize the wealth of knowledge I gained both inside and outside the classroom. But I think the most important lesson I learned was a fundamental shift in my life perspective: either I can be a part of someone else's world, or I can create my own and actually be the change. That value is priceless. Allow me to divulge further on the lessons I learned from my degree, and whether or not it was worth it. But don't worry, this advice won't cost you anything (except the price of the book; I guess nothing is truly priceless). As Len Schlesinger, the twelfth president of Babson once said to me, "I don't take myself too seriously. But I take my work very seriously."

One of the concepts they teach you early on is ROI (return on investment, or simply how much should I expect in return for risking capital, whether it be fiscal, social, political, etc.), and opportunity cost (What am I giving up in terms of time or other lost opportunities for committing to this project? What are my alternative options? Millennials would call this FOMO, or "Fear of Missing Out").

The opportunity cost of attending business school (or any graduate program) is extremely high; not only are you giving up two years of combined salary and potential job promotion if you're doing it full-time, but you also have to pay a lot of money for tuition. It's a double-whammy. But the flip side is that no one is forcing you to be there; you're surrounded by like-minded, highly motivated, and passionate students who are sacrificing a lot. Like anything in life, business school is what you make of it. You get out what you put in. The more you put into it, the more you get out of it. While it's true that just by attending you gain access to an incredible network of highly successful individuals, there is a lot more to be gained. It's not just a paper degree you need as a prerequisite to get high-paying jobs (unless you seek a job in finance, in which case you can make that argument; but for all other careers, you will actually need to know stuff).

So, what exactly do you learn by getting an MBA (Master of Business Administration)? A few things.

1. It instills an overall confidence in you. You're exposed to so many different financial and legal documents, nothing will be able to surprise you anymore. It doesn't mean you're an expert by any means, but it helps prepare you for whatever life may throw your way. It's important to have a basic understanding of financial documents (balance sheets, income statements, statements of cash flows) and how they're all interlinked.

2. "Entrepreneurial thought and action." This is Babson's motto, and it's an important one. At business school you'll learn that the most important thing you can do is take action. Don't be afraid to fail, because it's not really failure, anyway—you're just learning. We get so worried about public perception, judgment, and doubt that it can prevent us from accomplishing our goals.

I would argue that what business school really teaches you is a mindset: "I'm capable of creating change." It builds awareness. It teaches you to think objectively, remove emotion from the equation, and think of people as consumers. Stay at 30,000 feet. Stay focused on the prize. Identify problems and invest in human capital to fix them. Don't get involved in corporate bureaucracy and bullshit (don't worry about who gets the bigger desk; just focus on getting shit done). You must remain passionate about what you're doing. People start socially sustainable business models all the time. You must consistently ask yourself, "What are we trying to do?" Then do it.

Most importantly, don't do this if you don't love it. No one is around telling you what to do. It requires discipline, focus, and, above all, passion. You need to first ask yourself, "Why is this important to me?" and then, second, "Why me? Why, among all people, am I the right person to do this?" At the end of the day, no amount of classroom learning will replace real-life experience. However, you must first have the foundation of knowledge on which to build. And I can confidently say that without attending business school, I would have never been able to learn those lessons. It's easy to say these things and understand them conceptually, but it's an entirely different game to actually believe them in practice. That's the real value of your degree. That's what you're paying for.

TOP LESSONS LEARNED AS AN ENTREPRENEUR

With a near $2 million business education (between school tuition and some failed startups), I've picked up a few tips along the way that I thought I might share. Hopefully you can learn them a little bit more affordably than I did.

01

START SMALL AND GROW ORGANICALLY

Our ego gets in the way sometimes. When I built out my mansion-sized restaurant, I assumed the "if you build it, they will come" mentality. Not so. No matter how much hype you have prior to launch, things will take time. It takes time to build a loyal following. Months . . . years, even.

And if you have a celebrity endorsement and come out of the gates strong, you won't be ready for it! There are going to be product deficiencies, customer complaints, procedural errors, paperwork and hiring issues, etc. You're going to be so overwhelmed with pressure to perform and deliver on such high expectations, that you'll die of a heart attack before you ever get to enjoy any of it. So, be patient. Force yourself to start small, work out the kinks, and get customer feedback. Make the 1,000 little product adjustments that are necessary so that you'll be ready for the big leagues once you get called up. Don't force it through inflated promotion and unnecessary endorsements until you've gone through some trial and error.

02

DON'T SELF-FUND—EVEN IF YOU CAN

This is something they don't touch upon much in business school, probably due to the simple fact that most people can't entirely self-fund a concept. Unfortunately, I could. And I did.

Obviously, it's important to have skin in the game. Investors want to see that you're committed to your idea and putting at risk some of your own cash, not just theirs. That's fine. But put up a *tiny* amount. There is no pride or glory in financing a large majority of your business concept, no matter how much you believe in the idea. You're going to work hard *and* invest in your concept? That's crazy talk. Choose one: you're either the investor (in which case other people work their asses off for you to earn a return on your money) or you're the CEO (in which case you work hard for other people's money, with the hopes that you eventually get institutional investors and way more money than you could have put up yourself). But don't be both. Then you're working hard in order to spend and potentially lose money. Where's the glory in that?

03

IF YOU'RE GOING TO MAKE MISTAKES, MAKE THEM CHEAP

I'll give you a real-life example of an expensive mistake I made.

During the planning stages of my restaurant, I got excited about the idea of merging technology and food. I'd seen some major press about big chains like Chili's and TGI Fridays using iPads for customers to order directly from the table. It seemed very futuristic, convenient, and cool, and I thought it would create a ton of buzz.

I spent a lot of time and energy picking a point-of-sale system that had this new "self-ordering" iPad capability. There weren't many to choose from, and they were all expensive. But I really believed this would be a huge differentiator for me and was worth it. I settled on a new POS company based out of California and had them develop this beautiful user interface. More time and money.

It raised a whole new set of questions and challenges. How many iPads would we need to purchase? That's simple. One for every table. So, thirty. How would we deal with customer theft or employee theft? Two ideas: either we put an RF-tag on the back of each iPad (similar to a clothing store) and install a wireless fence, which would sound off an alarm if anyone tried to exit with it, or we lock them in a closet every night and have an employee checkout system for every shift. We decided to go with the latter. What about battery life? Can an iPad last an entire restaurant day (12+ hours), or do we now need to hire an electrician to install electrical outlets at every table? And once we do that, forget about being able to move tables around.

I hadn't even opened my doors yet, and already I was focused on things not relevant to my product, which was food. Was this really creating a customer solution to a problem? Or just creating more headaches for me? Long story short, I bought all these iPads (with an Apple Care protection plan for each, I might add) and installed them on the tables. As soon as we opened our doors, it became apparent that they were creating major operational issues in the kitchen, and customers didn't like them.

The key takeaway here is that this could have been easily avoided had we done the smart thing: launch a pilot program. Start with one or two iPads, have customers demo it, test it, and give feedback, then decide whether to move forward or not. Instead, we went full-scale right away. Huge mistake. We scrapped all the iPads after less than four weeks and liquidated them.

04

BUILD A TEAM YOU CAN TRUST, AND DON'T MICROMANAGE

Being a business owner as opposed to an employee of someone else's business is a unique experience hard to describe in words. No one will ever care as much as you do—for everyone else, it's simply a job. If your company goes down, they'll just go find another job. (Someone once told me, "It's always the rats that leave a sinking ship first.")

Also, most business owners tend to micromanage. How can you not? It's your baby. You want your hand in every part of the process. And there is nothing wrong with that. But in order to be successful, you can't spread yourself too thin. Everyone needs to have a clearly defined role and stay within that framework. When you become the business owner, you're no longer responsible for day-to-day operations. Instead, it's your job to make sure that everyone else is doing their job. Your attention needs to change to making sure other people are being held accountable. Which is why it's so important to have a management team you can trust.

I know it sounds cliché, but the challenge really is to find and retain top talent. How exactly do you find those people? This is where industry experience becomes a huge factor. The way you find those people is by having worked in that industry for a long time and seeing how people perform over a period of several years. Does this mean you shouldn't start

a business in an industry which you've never worked extensively before? No. But you will need someone who has. And whoever that person is needs to be properly vetted by you with references. Pick someone with results, someone who has a proven track record of success within the industry. This is not the time to be taking chances.

Once you build a team, you need to make sure everyone has skin in the game. This doesn't mean just handing them a piece of equity. They need to put up some cash as well. You can't be the only one losing something if the business fails.

05

DON'T START A HIGH FIXED-COST BUSINESS

On day one of business school you're told this. And here I am, the only idiot to start a high fixed-cost business.

Labor, rent, utilities, etc. Too much stress. Too little margin. Not scalable. It's 2019, not 1960. In today's digital world of e-commerce, there are so many ways to make money and distribute your product with less stress. This classic image of owning a local shop and supporting the family was nice a long time ago, but the world has changed since then, and you need to as well. You can open in new markets (both domestically and overseas) with the click of a button. Why restrict yourself to the 100-yard radius around your block and only make money during normal business hours? When you're online, you can be selling your product 24/7, 365 days a year. I know this sounds obvious, but people I talk to still aspire to own a shop or storefront. Do yourself a favor and lose that urge fast.

25

On Millennials

IT'S ONLY APPROPRIATE TO END THIS BOOK HOW WE STARTED. We've come full circle. Here are some departing thoughts, and the answer to the question on every old person's mind: "Are we screwed as a society?"

What does it mean to be a millennial "leader"? And can anyone become one? Being a leader means having a firm understanding of your beliefs and core values, independent of what others may think. It requires:

- mindfulness and compassion for others when making decisions

- consistency in your actions over a long period of time

- the ability to actively listen, without prepping for an immediate response; being free of judgment

- sensitivity to others' feelings

- the ability to detach yourself from bias and think objectively

- self-awareness, and the ability to self-analyze and self-critique, being honest about your strengths and weaknesses

- taking ownership and responsibility for your actions

- being open-minded about other's viewpoints, recognizing you don't always have the best ideas

- a wider perspective; not being so emotionally reactive; considering how things will be affected in months and years to follow, not minutes, days, and weeks from now— being careful before you commit to something; following through once you commit

Above all else, it's about what standard you set for yourself, irrespective of others' standards. Ask yourself, "How will I behave when no one is looking, when no one is there to hold me accountable?"

All of this requires a certain level of self-discipline, which millennials often lack. Millennials were born in a technologically transformative age. They want immediate gratification and expect everything to be "on demand" (including happiness). They tend to be hyper-sensitive; too much time on Instagram looking at a filtered view of the world has misled them to a phony, altered viewpoint of how people and the world actually work. What they fail to recognize is that other people will actually respect you *more*, not less, by sticking to your principles rather than trying to please everyone. It's okay to have ideological disagreements on how to pursue something. That is democracy. What's important is your reasoning "why" and the cogent logic behind it.

I believe any person has the capability of being a leader, but often people are too shortsighted in their viewpoints to build the respect necessary from others. It's a challenge to have the right temperament and balance of these qualities. Most people are incapable of finding that balance. I can assure you of one thing: without first having a strong sense of self, nothing else is possible.

Millennials love to challenge existing social norms. We're also the first generation to grow up without experiencing a military draft or large-scale global war. We've grown up in an age of comfort, technology, and industrialization. In this new digital world, there is a lot of good and bad to parse through.

The Bad: Millennials tend to use technology as a crutch to express their true feelings. We like to hide behind text messages. Because of this, basic communication skills are lacking, and millennials act surprised or impressed when someone truly expresses themselves IRL ("in real life"). Is this actually impressive? No, not really. It's just that no one is doing it. Millennials are obsessed with sharing and showing off. We're also very concerned about appearance; we're more worried about the *appearance* of accomplishment than *actual* accomplishment. We get caught up in this notion of perfection, which creates low self-esteem. It's a vicious, downward cycle.

The Good: Millennials ask the question, "Why? Why does it work like that? Why does it need to be done that way?" We challenge dated social mores. We got tired of being told to sit down and shut up. We got tired of being told we can't do something because "that's just the way it is." There are no more boxes, no more boundaries. Millennials will fight to the digital death for expressive freedom. Today, people are free to explore. Sexuality was publicly repressed, and millennials are changing that. Trans, poly, threesomes, open marriages, you name it. Gender identity is now in the open. Millennials (and the upcoming generation, Generation Z) are creating a more balanced and happier lifestyle.

Are we screwed as a society? Hardly. We're simply moving away from masochism and toward hedonism. We're evolving as a country. In my opinion, this can only be considered a good thing! I have no doubt that in fifty years, millennials will be sharing concerns about younger generations. In the meantime, let's enjoy the present for what it is.

CPSIA information can be obtained
at www.ICGtesting.com
Printed in the USA
LVHW081551240419
615091LV00028B/660/P